WAGES IN THE UNITED KINGDOM

IN THE NINETEENTH CENTURY.

WAGES

IN THE

UNITED KINGDOM

IN THE NINETEENTH CENTURY

NOTES FOR THE USE OF STUDENTS OF SOCIAL AND ECONOMIC QUESTIONS.

BY

ARTHUR L. BOWLEY, M.A., F.S.S.

LECTURER IN STATISTICS AT THE LONDON SCHOOL OF ECONOMICS AND POLITICAL SCIENCE.

CAMBRIDGE:
AT THE UNIVERSITY PRESS.
1900

CAMBRIDGE
UNIVERSITY PRESS

32 Avenue of the Americas, New York NY 10013-2473, USA

Cambridge University Press is part of the University of Cambridge.

It furthers the University's mission by disseminating knowledge in the pursuit of
education, learning and research at the highest international levels of excellence.

www.cambridge.org
Information on this title: www.cambridge.org/9781107419001

© Cambridge University Press 1900

First published 1900
First paperback edition 2014

A catalogue record for this publication is available from the British Library

ISBN 978-1-107-41900-1 Paperback

PREFACE.

THE following notes were originally prepared for the New-march Lectures at University College, London, in 1898; but since delivery they have been extended and entirely recast. Some apology is necessary for presenting this book in so unfinished a form, for in many cases it will be found that figures are left untabulated, and the means of solving a wage problem only suggested, when the solution itself might have been offered. My excuse is that the complete working up of the wage figures in any industry is an undertaking of considerable magnitude, which I am trying to carry out quarter by quarter in the *Statistical Journal*; and that, if I had waited till it was finished, many of the preliminary results, complete in themselves, would have been lost to those to whom they might be useful, and helpful criticism, which I trust may be evoked by these notes, lost to the author. It is hoped that in the course of no very long time it will be possible to extract from the wage records of the 19th century all that is essential, and to offer a more complete history of English wages. Meanwhile in the present volume an effort has been made to illustrate the various questions that arise in the study of wages, choosing those groups which afford problems of any special difficulty or interest; to show in some the work

in great detail, to indicate briefly in others the difficulties and
the way to overcome them, and in others to work up the
material to its final form.   Enough references have been given
in the text to enable any reader to verify most of the figures,
but in case of doubt use should be made of the bibliography
in Appendix III., and of the more complete one on the same
subject in the *Economic Review* of October, 1898.   These
notes would have been still less complete had it not been for
the constant co-operation of Mr George H. Wood of Bristol,
to whom my thanks are due not only for help with references,
material and writing, but also for the tables on Manchester
Cotton and Iron, which will be found to contain very satisfactory solutions of difficult problems.   My thanks are also
due to the Editors of the *Economic Journal* and to the
Council of the Royal Statistical Society for permission to use
work already published by them, and to Mr Sidney Webb
for valuable help in the compilation of Appendix II.

A. L. B.

December 1899.

TABLE OF CONTENTS.

SECTION I.

GENERAL OBJECT AND METHOD.

THE object of these notes is an examination of the recorded facts relating to wages in the United Kingdom during this century; it is not proposed to write the general history of wages, but to pass by questions of cause and effect, and of changes which appear to have resulted from specific events, and study only the numerical record of wages paid; in fact, underlying the purpose of these notes throughout are the purely arithmetical or statistical questions: What have been the total amounts and the averages of wages, and what the differences between trade and trade and from man to man, at the different epochs of this century, and what has been the progress of the wage-earning classes so far as it can be measured by the amounts of their earnings? Again, the object is not so much to give an *ex cathedrâ* estimate of these quantities, as to discuss the general nature of the problem, the material that exists for such estimates and its deficiencies, the various ways in which this material has been and can be handled, the exact meanings of the words—wages, earnings—and the special methods applicable for obtaining out of the scattered and vague data available accuracy and definiteness in the result. For the complete tabulation, classification and averaging of all the existing material the work of years would be necessary, and the results would be more suitable for a book of reference than for a student's manual; but it is hoped that a critical examination of the difficulties of investigations as to comparative wages, with tentative studies in some groups, together with a few

General object.

more exhaustive calculations, will prove of more use to students than mere pages of figures.

The following are the chief subjects that will be dealt with:—
Chief heads of treatment. the extent and nature of the material existing, and the chief authors and sources of information, with mention of some special difficulties in making general estimates; a general statistical history of the wages in groups of industries, such as agriculture, the building trades, mining, textiles, and mechanical engineering industries; the distinction between wages and earnings; the difficulties of conducting a wage census and former attempts to do so, and the special features of modern estimates; the more minute investigation of the wage-statistics of the building trades, illustrating the special difficulties which arise, and the methods of calculation applicable; the treatment of the statistics of a new and expanding trade, and of a decaying trade, the combination of these figures with the general average, and the difficulties in the way of a general comparison; and the reduction of all wage statistics to yearly averages referring to the whole sphere of industry.

The importance of wage-statistics can hardly be over-
Importance of the calcula-tion of money wages. estimated in relation to all investigations dealing with the welfare of the wage-earning classes, for, after all, the first thing to be determined in estimating the economic position of a working man, is the total amount of money he is able to earn during a year; and all other problems, such as the variation of the prices of commodities, the greater or less regularity of work, the amount of leisure, and the relative advantages of particular employments, though of very great importance, are still subsidiary, and their solution of little value till the money wage is known.

There are two general methods of dealing with wages *en masse*, which may be called respectively "statical"
The statical and kinetic methods of making com-parisons. and "kinetic." The "statical" is the method generally followed, and consists in making comprehensive estimates for given years, obtaining thus the average and distribution (i.e. the grouping of numbers of earners with respect to their wages at various distances from

the average) at those times, and finally comparing the results. This method is perfectly sound in theory, but is unfortunately difficult or impossible in practice. If we confined ourselves to it, we should only obtain three estimates, viz. those by Leone Levi, in 1866, 1878, and 1885, which we could compare with each other; and even modern material since 1886 would be difficult to handle. The other method, the "kinetic," which it is proposed to follow almost exclusively here, consists in studying not wages themselves, but their rates of change, making no attempt to construct a wage census for former dates or at the present time, but to study the proportionate changes of wages period by period, wherever we can obtain a sequence of figures, and combine the figures which indicate these rates of change independently of the actual rate of wages at any time or place. This method has the double advantage of making it possible to use all the material we have, and so to obtain comprehensive results, and also of bringing into play special causes, tending to an accuracy which the statical method lacks.

Using the kinetic method we can sometimes make use even of piece-rates; for if we know the piece-rates for a series of years we only need to know the time-rates for one year to deduce them for all, if we are justified in assuming that there has been no change in the method of production. This assumption is sometimes justified; for instance, in the minutes of the Hand-Loom Weavers' Commissions we find statements of piece-rates for 30 years or more, accompanied by evidence showing that neither pace, skill, nor machinery had greatly changed. With power-weaving it is very different; there we find a continued fall of piece-rates, increase of speed, and improved machinery, so that with the same or less labour the output continually increases: and in this case the change of piece-rates gives us no clue to the change of time-rates. Another example is found in modern cotton-spinning; here the piece-rates are continually adjusted, so that a given expenditure of labour of a certain degree of skill shall obtain given earnings in spite of adjustments of the machinery; while general changes are decided by a general increase or decrease per cent. on the piece-list prices. The methods are so complicated

The value of piece-rates in comparative estimates; and the prevalence of both piece- and time-rates.

that the workmen have to employ skilled officials to estimate
the rate of payment in conformity with the general agreement;
but we cannot be certain that a general percentage increase or
reduction, even when accepted by masters and workmen, and
applying to all piece-rates, bears an exact proportion to the
actual earnings; for the general process of development has
been that machines are continually "speeded up" (needing
more exertion on the part of the operative), or simplified and
improved (needing less exertion), to manufacture the same
product.   The recognised principle is to divide the extra
receipts due to these causes between men and masters, so that
if, for instance, there has been an improvement in machinery
increasing the output 10 per cent. for the same labour, we may
find 5 per cent. reduction in piece-rates, leaving the men an
increase of about 5 per cent. on their earnings; for the actual
calculation, however, it is necessary to get an estimate from
an expert thoroughly conversant with the trade. A confusion is
easily made when time- and piece-rates are paid in the same
trade, which is, indeed, the case in most trades where piece-
rates are general; thus many printers' compositors are paid by the
piece, so much per thousand letters, or sometimes per hundred
lines, but there are also many hands on the "'stab," i.e. with
weekly wages. These two groups of wages may be very different
from each other and change at different rates. In large iron-
works some men will always be paid at time-rates, either
because of special skill, as in the case of designers, or of
responsibility, as in the case of foremen or enginemen; and
even men doing work described under the same term may be in
some cases paid by time and in others by the piece. In such
cases it is never safe to assume that time- and piece-rates
change together and at the same rate.

This brings us to the question of the general usefulness of
different classes of information. Leaving aside
The value of
various kinds   questions of intentional bias, we may take it that
of information.
the statements of a casual observer outside the
trade are not of great value, for it can easily be discovered
by experiment that questions addressed informally to either
employers or workmen yield very vague results. Statements

of wages of an individual workman, of which many are extant, often show clearly his economic position and throw useful light on the influence of irregularity of employment, but it is more probable that individual peculiarities will be reflected than that any general information will be obtained; yet by combining a great many statements by workmen of the same class, such as are to be found in the earlier Commissions, we may obtain a fairly accurate average. We get on safer ground when there is a generally recognised scale of pay prevalent over a district, such as would be recognised in a law-court if no explicit contract had been made. This was commonly the case before the "industrial revolution," and owing to this fact it was possible for Thorold Rogers to collect sufficient material for *Six Centuries of Work and Wages.* It is still the case for many time-wages; for instance in the building trades the hourly rate is usually understood, in agriculture the customary rate of a district is easily found by local inquiry, and sailors are engaged at legally recognised rates. This fact adds value to the vast number of scattered statements found in books and reports of Commissions, when mention is made of rates prevalent in a trade with which they are not directly dealing. Again, we can often depend on the evidence of skilled observers who have made it their business to thoroughly understand all the circumstances of an industry, as for instance the agricultural sub-commissioners of the Labour Commission; and the summaries or reports of commissioners who have heard all there is to be said on all sides of the question have special value, except in the rare cases in which the evidence has been influenced by interested parties with a deliberate bias. Other series of trustworthy figures may be obtained from the records of institutions employing workmen occasionally, as for instance the celebrated list of wages paid at Greenwich Hospital, which has been quoted *ad nauseam* in default of any other series dealing with the same period.

The American method is to deal almost exclusively with records of wages paid to individual workers, which have been extracted from the books of manufacturers; the objections to this lie in the

American and English methods of collecting wage-statistics.

immense labour involved in making extracts, which leads
to carelessness or even falsification of statements, the incompleteness of the results obtained, and the impossibility of
following an individual for any length of time, owing to
frequent changes of employer. The English method adopted
in the "Wage Census" appears more satisfactory; there the
total wages paid in a given time are stated by manufacturers
directly from their books, together with the number of employés
and enough subsidiary information as to various rates of wages
to make a satisfactory survey of complete averages and distribution possible. The objections to this method lie simply in its
incompleteness; many manufacturers, presumably those who paid
the worst wages, made no returns, and many occupations were
omitted, while casual or unattached labour hardly came within
the cognizance of the Census. The following rule is important
in this connection: in every statement of wages, in addition
to the place and date, the source of the information should be
known, and also the object with which it was made, and the
extent of the district and trade which it is intended to cover.

It is perhaps hardly necessary to mention that account
must be taken of many additions to and deduc-
Difference
between nomi-   tions from wages, and that the effect of change of
nal wages and
actual earn-   custom on the relation between gross and net
ings.
earnings and on payments in kind must be borne
in mind in comparative statements extending over a series of
years. The deductions include necessary payments for assist-
ance in work, rent of machinery, payment for light, tools, oil,
gunpowder, &c.; fines for bad work or breach of rules—sometimes amounting to a regular tax—and expense of getting to
work; there are others less easy to reckon, and theoretically,
perhaps, not entering into the question, such as compulsory
deduction for insurance, specially high house-rent due to the
necessity of living in a special district, specially high prices of
commodities, those concealed extortions which have been
diminished by the Truck Acts, expense of special clothing or of
an arbitrarily high standard of living, all of which come under
the economic question of real income, rather than the statistical question of wages. The additions are:—payments in kind,

which have gradually diminished throughout the century, and vitiate simple comparisons of money wages ; free board, free house or ground, free clothes, cheap coals or free haulage, special facilities for cheap purchase without middlemen's profits, bonuses, or special opportunities for earning extra money for special tasks. One of the advantages of the "kinetic" method is that errors from such causes are diminished in comparison; if workmen state their earnings too low in one year, they may be expected to do so in another; if manufacturers give wages of their most skilled or steadiest workmen at one time, they will take the same optimistic view at another; if we have taken too limited a view and recorded the wages of a special instead of those of an average set of men, we are still likely to find the same rate of increase with them as with the general run of workmen; if we have omitted fines and necessary disbursements throughout, our ratio is only affected if they have, relatively to wages, increased or diminished; if we have not been able to estimate payment in kind, perquisites or valuable facilities, our omission has less effect in a comparison than in a single estimate and shows only an exaggerated increase, perhaps capable of correction, due to the substitution, always gradual, of money for kind. The effect, in fact, of all bias is diminished, and so long as we confine ourselves to estimates made on the same principle, not, for instance, comparing a workman's statement for one year with an employer's for another, by the use of the "kinetic" method we avoid very many of these errors.

It appears at first sight to be more logical to consider family earnings rather than the wage of single men ; to imagine a typical family with a definite number of wage-earners of different ages and to calculate what they could jointly earn at different

Wages of single men to be preferred to family earnings.

periods, places or trades; but, though many interesting estimates exist for special times and places, this is impracticable on any large scale. It is not evident, moreover, that this method gives a better criterion of the position of the working-classes than the simpler plan of estimating the earnings of an ordinary man in full work in the prime of life; for it is very difficult to balance the advantages of facilities for child labour against the resulting lack of education and hindrance to natural development, and it is questionable on which side of the account the effect of work by married women should be placed; it is even doubtful whether the opportunities of earnings presented to boys in a large town are an advantage.

This brings us to the very difficult question of women's

Women's wages.

wages — difficult because the conditions have changed immensely during the century; on the one hand the opportunities of fairly well-paid work having developed, on the other the available supply of labour having increased; difficult also because so great a mass of women's wages are not paid according to the unrestricted action of the laws of supply and demand; and difficult, finally, because the

Apprentices.

records are so meagre. The difficulty of the whole problem is increased by the apprentice system, with the rapidly changing rates paid at different ages and the variations of the age at which full wages begin to be paid. For these reasons it seems desirable to confine our attention for the present to the wages of adult males, and to postpone the consideration of the more complex question of family earnings.

The question of hours of work is best treated separately

Simplification of problem by reserving for separate treatment:
i. hours of work,

from that of wages. For separate trades, indeed, the statement that in one year a certain amount was earned for so many hours' work, in another a greater amount in fewer hours, may give complete information; but for a general estimate it is futile to try to work out the hourly rate in order to make comparisons year by year, if only because an hour's work varies so much in intensity.

Another problem, fitted for separate investigation, is that of

ii. irregularity of work,

the amount of irregularity of employment. There is, perhaps, no good reason for thinking that this has changed much for better or for worse in any part of the century, apart from the general fluctuations due to inflation and depression of trade which affect in particular the coal and iron industries; at any rate, any attempt to apply a factor representing regularity of work to each separate statement of wages would be futile. It is preferable to aim at such a statement as the following:—since a certain date the average wage has increased 20 per cent., so that the average annual wage of fully employed adult male workmen in a normal season, then £50, is now £60, and in the same period the average duration of the week's work has diminished from 65 to 57 hours.

To simplify the problem yet further, it is best to aim first at calculating the change in the average, and afterwards to consider the distribution of wage-earners according to their earnings about this average. *iii. distribution about the average.* It would, of course, be possible that the average should have risen through exceptionally high earnings on the part of a few highly skilled men, while a larger section was falling into poverty; but, if we attempt to pay attention to this in the course of our calculations, we shall only hopelessly complicate our working. Having found our average, which, as is always the case with averages, carries us only a little way, it is then time to study the distribution about it, to find how many men earn wages within a certain distance of the average, how many far below it, and how many are in receipt of really considerable wages; and, if we leave out of account paupers and casual workmen, as fitter subjects for special investigation, it will perhaps be possible to obtain ultimately at least a partial solution of this further problem.

SECTION II.

NATURE OF MATERIAL AND CHIEF AUTHORITIES.

IT is commonly said that the material for wage-statistics is conspicuous by its absence, and most authors who need such figures to illustrate other subjects are content to quote one or two estimates covering a very small part of the field; even Mr Mulhall, who has found statistics of almost every measurable quantity, is obliged to give very few figures of wages.

The extent and unsatisfactory nature of material existing for wage-estimates.

It is not true, however, that wage-figures do not exist, even in the case of England; for since 1886 at least there has been a great abundance of official material, while there is no scarcity of books and reports throughout the century dealing with special parts of the subject, and a great number of shorter pamphlets and tracts and many books devoting a short section to wages are in existence; but above all there are official publications and reports of commissions for the past hundred years, very many dealing directly with the condition of the working classes, while others, dealing primarily with administrative or commercial subjects (for instance, factory inspectors' reports), contain wage-figures incidentally, and to complete the examination of these it would be necessary to overhaul some 5000 volumes, each of 500 to 1000 pages. Besides these there are the journals of economic societies, and a library of reports of Trade Unions and of working-class or other newspapers. The fact is that the material is superabundant, and it is scarcely possible to give even a cursory glance at it all in any reasonable time; but its usefulness is not commensurate with its magnitude, for it is discursive, fragmentary, tediously full in some particulars, hopelessly lacking in others.

There have often been serious attempts to calculate the wages in particular trades, occasionally in parti- Former cular towns, more rarely all over the country. estimates for special in-The hand-loom weavers, for instance, formed the dustries, subject of thousands of pages of Government publications and other books, and their complaint was satisfactorily diagnosed for a dozen years, while they themselves were starving on 7 s. a week, and by the date of the Commission of 1838 had nearly ceased to exist; textile wages have so considerable a literature, that, but for the inherent difficulties in dealing with these wages in particular, their complete history could well be written; agricultural wages have always been a favourite theme with statisticians, and have formed the subject, incidentally at least, of many Commissions and Select Committees. In some occupations, on the other hand, the material is useless or totally lacking; of these the most important are the boot and shoe manufacture, the employment of domestic servants and shop-assistants, and such home industries as tailoring; and the records of railway-servants' wages are very deficient.

When we come to combine estimates of different trades to obtain a view of the statistical whole, we are in yet greater difficulties. We find, for instance, lists and difficulty of combining of wages in Manchester in 1859 and 1884, while them. for London we only have estimates for 1871 and 1894; we have statistics for mines in 1845 and 1870, for agriculture in 1860 and 1870. Even if we confine our view to a single trade we find records for such a series of dates as 1833, 1839, 1849, 1859, 1870, 1877, 1883, 1886, and 1893 with a series of ratios in one branch from 1823 to 1833, and with no means of filling the gaps. The material may be compared with that with which geologists have to be content. Here they find a broken fossil, there a superabundance of an allied species, and a continuous record through several strata, then fresh gaps; from these they must describe the flora and fauna of different continents throughout the geological periods. Yet their task is simpler in one respect than ours, in that their records are true; whilst with respect to

Unreliability of most wage-statements. wages most observers are incompetent, do not register the essential facts, or describe incompletely what they do register ; so that in a statement of the wages of an agricultural labourer, for instance, the free cottage or free beer is omitted, or a weaver's rent for his loom, or a spinner's payment to his piecers, either are not deducted or we are left in doubt as to whether they are included or not. Still worse, many books are written in a biassed spirit ; highest wages are given as the average, ill-paid trades are not noticed, and no allowance is made for normal lost time, when the object is to show the prosperity and unfounded discontent of the working classes ; while a newspaper correspondent in search of a sensation, or a politician of popularity, will produce a sombre view by exclusive attention to the worst paid labourers or to decaying trades ; and such bias is found even in the evidence offered to Government commissions.

The search for wage-statistics. The actual search for these statistics is most interesting, even exciting ; it is not possible to judge from the title of a book on trade or on the " state of the people " whether wage-statistics are to be found there or not ; for instance, in one book of 400 pages on the *Condition of the Irish Poor* wages are only once given, and there too vaguely to be of any use. At another time in turning through the journal of a Trade Union, after years dealing with only rules, subscriptions and officers, we may suddenly find a complete list of trade wages throughout the kingdom, or even a systematic account of wages for a period of 50 years. The search for a missing book, to which a reference has been found, will often take the student to library after library, and it may be found as a pamphlet in a working-class newspaper, or perhaps prove to be a mere copy of some better known work. An account of wages for a particular year may at last come to light in an incidental reference in a book on some other subject. Much time is wasted, for after a laborious compilation from a detailed account it may often be found that the whole has been ably summarised and analysed by some author not yet examined ; this is especially the case with Reports of Parliamentary Commissions, which are often summarised and indexed in their final report, and have formed not infrequently the subject of a treatise especially devoted to their results, rendering reference to the originals almost unnecessary. In searching for material the general aim to keep in view is the discovery of sequences of figures, the most valuable being those compiled by a single authority from similar records for a series of years.

The method to be followed here will be to study wages, trade by trade; but before proceeding to this it will be well to notice the most important of the general estimates made by competent statisticians of wages of their times, the few general comparative estimates, and the better known authorities on the wages of different industries.

For wages at the end of the last century Eden's *State of the Poor* should be consulted. He, though dealing chiefly with agricultural wages, mentions also those of carpenters and masons, and less frequently of ironworkers, miners, and manufacturers, in their chief districts, his method being to state wages, county by county, through England and Wales. Arthur Young's plan is similar, but more strictly confined to agriculture: his investigation extends to Ireland, and over a series of years up to 1809.

Brief review of chief authorities.

Next we should mention Tooke, who, while stating very few actual wage-figures in his *History of Prices*, gives many indications of the course of wages which may serve to check results obtained from other sources. The same remark applies to the Annual Supplement contained in the February number of the *Economist* newspaper, entitled *Commercial History and Review*, from 1863 onwards. Passing by Colquhoun's short general estimate of national income and wages in *A Treatise on Indigence* in 1806, we come to a group of books dealing with the early history of textiles, e.g. Ure's *Philosophy of Manufactures* and his *Cotton Manufacture of Great Britain*, both continued by Simmonds. *The History of Cotton*, by E. Baines, contains an important table of wages in Manchester, 1810—1832, with prices of food and necessaries, which are given also in the *British Almanack and Companion* of 1834. There are also two general charts to be found in the library of the Royal Statistical Society dealing with early dates, by Layton Cooke, and by

Britten, representing wages from 1760 to 1826 and 1760 to 1845 respectively. Neither of these, however, is complete, nor based on reliable information.

The *Gorgon*, a working-class newspaper published in 1819, affords a few lists of consecutive wages of special trades due to Francis Place; Symon's *Arts and Artisans at Home and Abroad* gives general but discursive figures for 1810—1839. Tuckett in *The Past and Present State of the Labouring Population* is disappointing; he states very few figures and none of them are original. Proceeding in chronological order we come to the next classic dealing exhaustively with the subject, viz. Porter's *Progress of the Nation*; besides quoting the best authorities for special trades, he gives a table showing all the authentic lists of wages which he could find relating to various occupations from 1800 to 1836; further tables due to him are to be found in the *Statistical Journal* of 1850. McCulloch's *Statistical Account of the British Empire* contains only a few tables, but these are very good. Brassey, whose various papers and lectures are contained in four volumes[1], gives many details of wages, chiefly relating to railways, iron and coal, between the dates 1840 and 1870.

Among books referring to special districts we have as early as 1835, *A Journey throughout Ireland*, by Inglis, whose investigations resemble Eden's in England at an earlier date. Strang[2] gives detailed wages in many trades in the West of Scotland, especially in Glasgow in the fifties; Chadwick[3] tabulates a very comprehensive series of wages in Manchester in 1839, 1849, and 1859, the most exhaustive list for any district published up to that date. There may be mentioned in passing, as an illustration of useful statistics well concealed from the casual inquirer, a series of newspaper articles, the author and the name of the paper unknown, only to be found, so far as I know, in Prof. Foxwell's library, which give interesting details of wages paid in Edinburgh and Leith in the first half of this century.

---

[1] *Vide* p. 140.
[2] *Stat. Soc. Journal*, 1857 and 1858.
[3] *Ib.*, 1860.

There are many Parliamentary reports referring both to these and to later dates, with discursive information as to wages in all trades and throughout the country. A list of the most important of these is to be found in the appended Bibliography (p. 139), which forms a list of the books containing wage-statistics most important to students.

The *Report on Trade Societies* of the National Association for the Promotion of Social Science, in 1860, contains a few lists of figures, unfortunately much scattered both as regards dates and districts. Coming to more recent dates we have elaborate and exhaustive estimates of total wages by Baxter[1], in 1869, and Leone Levi[1], in 1867 and 1885; a very general account of the *Progress of the Working Classes* for 50 years by Sir Robert Giffen in his *Essays on Finance*[2], which, depending on the most reliable information, obtains interesting general results. This essay, indeed, forms the best classic for a student beginning the study of the subject, showing, as it does, the difficulties of making estimates and their value when made. In it there is reference to a paper by Montgomery, comparing wages in Manchester in 1834 and 1884, published in the Manchester Statistical Society's Journal, 1884, in which Journal is also to be found Mertten's continuation to 1893 of Ure's and Chadwick's figures, so far as cotton wages in Manchester are concerned. Very general information for the years 1876—1885 is given in certain American reports, but the amount of reliability to be placed on the figures and averages there published is varying and doubtful, and comparison of these estimates with each other or English publications is difficult; the chief of these is Edward Young's *Labour in England and America*; Schoenhof's *Industrial Situation*, 1885, also gives useful general comparisons over long intervals.

I have already summarised most of the available statistics from 1860 to 1891 in the *Journal of the Royal Statistical Society* of 1895, and since the methods I am here using are a development of those there employed, and my present calculations will refer chiefly to dates before those of my former paper, it would be well if readers acquainted themselves with that article. It

---

[1] *Vide* pp. 65—70.   [2] Second Series.

will be seen that in it much reliance is placed on the *Returns of Wages from* 1830 *to* 1886[1], which contains all that was published by the Statistical Department of the Government between those dates, and is in fact the only official book up to 1886 dealing exclusively with wages. Reference is also made to the *Reports on Trade Unions* to the Board of Trade, of which the most important for the present purpose is the 4th for 1891, which contains practically all the lists of wages extending over a series of years published in any of the reports up to the present date. The basis of the final calculation in that paper is what is known as the Wage Census of 1886 to 1891, which is the only reliable general estimate in existence, but does not in reality cover the whole ground. The Labour Department has taken up the work in its *Standard Time- and Piece-Rates*, and in its annual publications of *Changes of Wages and Hours of Labour*, which are also published monthly in the *Labour Gazette* and summarised briefly each year in the *Annual Report of the Labour Department.*

Most of the books mentioned so far are easily obtained at the British Museum or any other good library (with the exception of the Parliamentary papers, of which few complete series are in existence), but the history of wages must be sought to a great extent in records of Trade Unions. These records have often not been preserved at all, since the officials of Trade Unions are generally too busy, or with too little sympathy for the requirements of historical research, to form a library of their own publications, many of which are indeed of only ephemeral interest, and very few of them find their way to the British Museum. There are, however, many societies which have issued for several years full reports both of their private business and of the contemporary history of their trade. Some publish annually, or frequently, lists of the wages recognised by the society in all its districts. In dealing with these it must be remembered that the wages recognised are not the same thing as the wages paid, both because they only apply necessarily to the members of the Union, who may be only a minority of all employed, and

The records of Trade Unions.

[1] Referred to hereafter as *Returns of Wages.*

because they often represent the standard which the Union desires to establish, rather than the wages actually paid. It should be noticed also, that the wages are only the minimum which a workman is allowed by his Trade Union rules to accept, and that skilled men often earn much more than this rate; moreover, when overtime is at all common in an employment, wages may rise considerably above the given standard. These records have recently become accessible to students through the energy and generosity of Mr and Mrs Sidney Webb, who, after collecting practically all the literature of Trade Unions of which duplicates could be found in Trade Union Offices, and using them for their works on the *History of Trade Unionism* and *Industrial Democracy*, have presented the collection to the British Library of Political Science, where it is now in course of arrangement[1]. These records are mostly confined to the more recent years, many being complete only in very recent times; but some, for instance those of the Maidstone paper-makers, go back to early in this century, and a few trades, especially printers' compositors, were strongly united even at the end of the last century, and their records are preserved. The earlier lists of wages are unfortunately often confined to piece-work statements, and it is still the case that it is far more difficult to find the amount of earnings in trades where piece-rates are the rule, than in others; thus, we have elaborate rates for cabinet work from 1800 onwards, but it is quite impossible to deduce from them how much any individual earned in a given time, and the same remark applies to the tailoring and boot and shoe manufacturing industries up to the present date.

[1] This library is open freely to all *bonâ fide* students: 10, Adelphi Terrace, London, W.C.

SECTION III.

MEANING AND USE OF "THE AVERAGE WAGE."

AT first sight, when we look at the great variety of occupations at all ages, the different capacity of various
The average wage as a measure of wages in general. workers, and the immense difference between the wages of persons apparently of the same skill, it does not appear that the wages of members of the population are related to one another by any law, and it seems absurd to speak of an average change; for it is only reasonable to speak of an average of things which possess close resemblance one to another, and the wages of different individuals of the working class do not appear to be more nearly allied to each other than they are to the incomes of the wealthy or professional classes. On closer investigation, however, it will be found that in spite of this apparent want of connection between the wages of one class of men and another, there are very distinct causes
Law of equality of wages, and its limits. which tend to make the following law hold:—at the same time and in the same place the wages for equal effort of men of the same capacity are equal to one another; or more generally, the wages throughout the country for equal degrees of skill, are equal at any given time. If this is so, we shall find it useful to watch the change of the rate of wages paid for a certain degree of skill, even though the number of persons paid at this wage may be a very small proportion of the total number doing similar work. This principle of equal payment for work requiring the same capacity and effort is recognised very generally; according to Mr and Mrs Webb[1] the standard rate is the chief aim of Trade Union

---

[1] *Industrial Democracy*, Part II., Chap. v.

regulations; it is not the Trade Unionist's object to obtain equal wages for all members of his Society, as is often erroneously asserted, but to arrange wages by piece or time, as the case may be, in such a way that men of equal skill shall obtain the same wage, whatever their class of work, and men of less or greater skill, a less or greater wage. This is the case in particular in cotton spinning, where every slight alteration of machinery involves a difference in the amount of effort required for a given amount of work ; an increase in the number of spindles or a quickening of the mechanical actions increases the strain on the operative, and for this compensation must be made by a corresponding increase of wage. The principle is therefore consciously adopted in very many instances, and in trades where this is the case we are justified in taking the wage of one person as the representative of all. The principle holds also as between trade and trade; the more skilled the workman, the smaller is the number of his competitors, and the higher the wage he will be able to obtain ; if he cannot find this higher wage in his own trade he will, if *Fluidity of labour.* possible, change to another; but though the regulation according to degrees of skill is very rapid and effective in a single large workshop, or throughout a whole industry, especially one that is organised, it is not so rapid when an alteration of a man's trade has to be made to bring it about. In the first place, when a man has once chosen his employment, it is, generally speaking, very difficult for him to change to another ; and in the second place a choice of a trade is determined not so much by a nice weighing of all possible advantages and disadvantages, and a careful estimate of the pay corresponding to different grades of skill, as by general impressions and the force of circumstances. The tendency therefore to bring about uniformity of wages for equal degrees of skill is subject to a considerable amount of what is called economic friction. On looking through the average wages in different trades throughout the century it will be seen that the law of equality of remuneration has had certain play ; it has been the case that when wages have fallen, or not risen so much as the general average *Examples of diminution of numbers in industries where wages are low or increasing slowly.*

2—2

throughout an industry, the numbers in that industry have decreased. Perhaps the best example is the case of the hand-loom weavers, for as the prices of hand-work dropped owing to the competition of machinery, all the weavers who could find any other occupation left their original employment; very many in Scotland, for instance, took to agriculture or market gardening, and no young persons entered the trade. A fairly close relation has been found by Mr Hooker[1], between the wages and numbers of those employed in coal mines in recent years. The general migration from country to town affords another example; it will be found that agricultural wages have not increased with the same rapidity as average wages, and that the numbers of the agricultural population have been very nearly stationary, instead of increasing: indeed, if a list is written down of the trades whose numbers have increased more than the average, and of those trades whose numbers have decreased, or increased less than the average, it will be found that in general the wages of the former are precisely those wages which have increased more than the average wage and vice versâ[2].

Let us consider further the relation between the average wage and the wages of the community. In any large group of men it is obvious that differences will be found in ability, but it is not so well understood that the distribution of numbers in different degrees of ability is to some extent invariable. This subject has been worked out by Mr Galton[3], and the result he arrives at may be roughly stated as follows: suppose it possible to measure ability as height is measured; the great majority will be found with nearly the average ability; as you rise above, or go beneath the average, you find fewer and fewer instances according to a regular law. In the case of height, the law is so regular, that it is possible to deduce almost with certainty the entire distribution of the heights of a large population when the average is known. Laws of grouping appear to hold universally for all

The distribution of wages about their average.

[1] *Statistical Journal*, 1894.
[2] *Vide Econ. Journal*, Sept., 1896, p. 469.
[3] *Vide Hereditary Genius.*

physical measurements, and there is reason to Hypothesis that this distribution is regular.
believe that degrees of mental activity are dis-
tributed in a similar way. If we could estimate
this average of skill, and also discover any rule by which wages
changed according to degrees of skill displayed, we could at
once proceed to find the general grouping of wages about the
average. Though this is not possible in general, yet, bearing
in mind this ideal case, it will be seen that if we know the
distribution of wages for different degrees of skill at any one
date, we may reasonably expect that the distribution at any
other date will be similar; that, in fact, the supply of skill is
regular, and the gradation of rates of pay regular. This will be
true except in the case in which there has been a general change
in education and consequently in the supply of skill, or when
the facility of obtaining skilled occupation has generally increased or diminished, or if there has been a general cause
affecting the demand for different degrees of skill, as would be
the case, for instance, if the introduction of machinery meant
that a lower degree of skill was required from the operative.
This is only another way of stating that the supply of labour is
in general similarly grouped as to quality, but if from general
causes one class has increased more than another (as if, to
return to our simile, a new diet had influenced height), or if
the demand for a special degree of skill has diminished, the
distribution of wages will be affected. This brief discussion
shows the hypothesis of a regular or normal distribution about
an average both of skill and wages to be reasonable, especially
when the comparison extends over only a short period.

Facing p. 22 is given an example of such distribution relating
to a great number of wage-earners. The vertical Example of such distribution.
lines are proportional to the numbers receiving
the daily rates of pay stated on the lower hori-
zontal line. If there is a law of wages, the shape of the figure
formed by joining the tops of the vertical lines should be
regular for different groups or periods. The dotted line shows
a similar distribution when only half of the whole group is
taken. If the shape of the figure is regular, it is only necessary
to know a few points on it to trace the rest: we need only

know, for instance, the greatest, the least, and the average; or the average and the limits within which half the group may be found.

How, then, should we determine the average workman?

Discussion of the special average to be employed. The most natural method of procedure would be to calculate the total paid in wages, the number of wage-earners, and by division the average wage, and to say that the man who received the average wage was the average workman; but there are other methods which are both simpler and better adapted for our purpose. The first is to find, not what are the average wages, but what is the wage most frequently paid, technically called

The 'mode.' the $mode^1$. In the larger group in the diagram it is between $1\frac{1}{4}$ and $1\frac{3}{4}$\$. Determine the position of the mode for a series of years, and assuming that the shape of the curve does not change, it can be constructed for each successive year from the knowledge of this single point on it.

The statement actually determined by this method will be that "the wage which was paid to the greatest number of workmen was in 1800, 15s. per week, and in 1890 a wage of 25s.," or whatever the figures might prove to be. This method has the disadvantage that we may find more than one such maximum position; for if we follow a list of wages we often find that a great number are grouped at the wage paid to ordinary unskilled labour, and another great number at the wage paid to skilled labour.

The other method is that of finding the *median* wage-earner; that is the man whose wage is such that

The 'median' equal numbers of men are paid at rates above and below that wage, so that if all workers were ranged in order according to the amount of their wages he would occupy the middle point of the line. In the two figures the

and 'deciles.' median wages are 1·70 and 1·55\$. We can also proceed to determine the man whose place would be $\frac{1}{4}$ and $\frac{3}{4}$ or $\frac{1}{10}$, $\frac{2}{10}$, $\frac{3}{10}$ and so on, down the line; this is Mr Galton's

---

[1] Arrange all the wage-earners in groups, as receiving between ·75 and 1·25\$, between 1·25 and 1·75\$, &c.; the group which contains the greatest number of persons is at the *mode*; the exact position of the mode cannot be easily determined in wage statistics, but must be given as within certain limits as in the text.

method of *deciles*.   These deciles in the smaller figure are
at ·95, &c.   It may often be fairly easy to calculate these, and
their determination gives us almost all the information we are
in search of; for given 9 points on a curve it is generally
possible to construct it with reasonable accuracy.

In lists of wages in the latter half of the last century it was
very frequently the case that wage-earners were *Artisans and*
divided simply into two classes, labourers and *labourers.*
mechanics, at wages perhaps of 1*s.* 3*d.* and 2*s.* 6*d.* a day
respectively.   For instance, Tuckett gives: weekly wages of

	Agricultural labourers.	Artisans.
1780	8*s.*	16*s.*
1810	14*s.* 6*d.*	30*s.*
1840	11*s.*	33*s.*,

With this may be placed a statement from the Poor Law
Reports of 1861, viz., labourers 15*s.*, artisans 30*s.* in London.
During the evolution of machine manufacture the modern
subdivision of labour into its numerous classes has proceeded
so rapidly, that it is no longer always possible to label a
particular man categorically as skilled or unskilled.   There is
still to a certain extent, however, the distinction between the
man who has learned a trade,—called in Trade Union language
a "journeyman" or "tradesman"—and the man who does only
unspecialized work, and it is still the case that in any large
workshop there will be found two groups of men corresponding
to these two classes; for instance, a blacksmith has his striker,
a bricklayer his labourer, a rivetter his holder-up, a plumber
his mate, and an erector his labourer; and it may be noticed
that when a diagram is made representing the grouping of wage-
earners according to their wages, its shape indicates this fact.
Thus in the diagram facing p. 22 there are signs of a group at
3·50$, especially visible in the lower line; while in Mr Booth's
London[1] distinct groups are to be found at 20*s.* and at 35*s.*
It may therefore prove to be possible to consider *The method*
the change in average wages of skilled and un- *of procedure.*

---

[1] e.g. *Life and Labour of the People*, Vol. x. p. 371, and elsewhere.

skilled workmen separately; and if we can further obtain an idea of the change of wages of the median man, of the average man, of the greatest group and of the most skilled, we shall have gone a very long way towards determining not only such a vague quantity as the average change, but also the much more definite quantity—the actual distribution about this average. How far this can be carried out for any particular period or group depends entirely on the nature of the information; so far as I know it has never yet been attempted.

SECTION IV.

AGRICULTURAL WAGES IN ENGLAND.

IT is proposed next to consider the material that exists for constructing a complete table of agricultural wages throughout the century.

From the tables (see pp. 29, 30 and at end) which summarize the information as to the ordinary weekly wages of agricultural labourers, it will be seen that there have been nine dates from 1795 to 1892, at each of which there has been a general investigation of agricultural wages. A preliminary column is given for 1767—70, both because it is generally quoted and because our next period, 1793–5, is one of rapid change, so that the exact date to be assigned to an average, or an average to a date, is open to a little doubt. For this period we have first incomplete statements scattered through Arthur Young's writings; a more complete statement from Eden's *State of the Poor,* and for comparison a few figures from Davies' *Case of Labourers in Husbandry.* For Eden and Young's estimates, investigations were made in each county to determine the prevailing rate of wages, while Davies' results are simply the average of a few detailed cases sent to him, apparently by personal friends from districts where they lived.

The figures for the next period for which the list is complete, 1824, were extracted from the report of the *Select Commission on Labourers' Wages* by taking the average of a long list of wages prevailing in separate

The information available.

Young, Davies, and Eden.

The Commission of 1824.

villages or districts in each county—a purely mechanical method, differing from that of Young and Eden, in that they often stated the prevailing county rate from direct observation and study of details, and so avoided possible errors from the inclusion of unreasonably high or low figures. To give examples from 1824, the only figures for Huntingdonshire are 8s., and 5s. to 9s.; in default of further information we must simply take

the average (7s. 6d.), and mark it doubtful. In Essex the figures are 9s. to 10s., 6s. to 9s., 10s. to 12s., 9s., 9s., 9s. to 12s., 8s. to 9s., and 8s. to 10s.

Peculiarities of agricultural wages.

The double figures mean that in the same districts some were paid at the higher and some at the lower wage. In special cases it may happen that there is a preponderance at the higher or at the lower rate, or that the higher figure only refers to a few special cases; but generally it will mean that both rates are general, since otherwise the most common only would be given, and the average must be between the two rates, probably nearly half-way. Notice further that the longer the list the less chance there is of one exceptional or erroneous rate influencing the average; thus if in the second group in Essex the 6s. was only paid to one man, and should therefore be excluded, while others were from 8s. to 9s., the average for the county would only be altered by 1d.

The list for Devon shows special points; it is as follows:—
8s., 7s., 6s., 8s., 9s., 7s., 7s. to 9s., 6s. to 9s., 8s., 6s. to 7s., 8s. to 9s., 7s., 6s. to 9s.; and four groups—6s. to 8s., 8s., 7s., 7s. to 8s.— where liquor is stated to have been given in addition to wages. A glance along the figures shows their average to be 7s. Now it was very general and is not yet uncommon to provide labourers with drink, generally with home-brewed beer or cider. The question with regard to every wage stated on the pages is whether drink was given but is not mentioned, not given, given and mentioned, or whether a valuation is included in the wage. In the earlier lists, at any rate, no valuation is included; very frequently the fact was not mentioned, drink being only one of many perquisites to which the labourer is customarily entitled, and not properly included in his money wage. It is improbable that the custom would vary within a

small district, and it is otherwise known that providing drink was common in Devon. The conclusion is that the simple average of the figures represents weekly wages excluding drink, but that in attempting an estimate of annual earnings an allowance (of 1s. or so a week) should be made. It is not uncommon for the farmers to provide one or two meals a day, and this practice varied from county to county, farm to farm, and even man to man, but in this case the fact is generally mentioned; thus wages in Derbyshire and Leicestershire in 1793 were 6s. and food. It is often possible to estimate the value of the food by comparing wages where it was with those where it was not included. In some cases accidental omission, due to defective information, or mistakes in tabulating, may account for phenomenally low wages, as for example, 6s. in Devon, and correction can hardly be made for this. In other instances, chiefly in Westmoreland, Cumberland, a large part of Wales, and the greater part of Scotland, labourers are boarded and lodged by the farmer; when this is the case no statement of weekly wages can in general be made, though some figures are given relating to exceptional labourers who are so paid, and whose net advantages and earnings are probably the same as others living at the farm.

The next group of figures belongs to the period 1832-8, when several investigations were made in con- *The Com-* nection with the effect of the sliding-scale duties *missions of* on corn and the cause of the commercial depres- *1832—38.* sion of 1836—42. When tabulated these figures give fairly extensive information for 1832-3, while a very detailed report of the Poor Law Commissioners furnishes a complete list, county by county, in 1833. A further list for 1837 is obtained from Mr Purdy's paper in the *Statistical Journal* of 1861.

For the latter half of the century we have a very reliable estimate by Caird for 1851, and in 1860-1 and *Caird and* 1869—70 official returns were made of the pre- *the Returns* vailing rates of wages, county by county. The *of 1860 to 1870.* first column for 1860-1 is taken directly from the *Returns of Wages*; thus for Surrey the wages given are:

Michaelmas 1860 : 12s., 14s.   Av. 13s.

Christmas 1860 : 12s., 13s.   ,, 12s. 6d.

Ladyday   1861 : 12s., 12s. 9d.   ,, 12s. 4½d. Av. 12s. 7d.

Midsummer (interpolated)   ,, 12s. 4½d.

The assumption for Midsummer is necessary to complete the
year, and is justified by a study of the corresponding returns for
1870–1, where the Midsummer wage is generally found to be
very near that of Ladyday.

Villiers and Purdy made contemporary estimates based on
these returns adjusted by their personal knowledge of agriculture, and Hasbach quotes from them. The two are placed
side by side to show that slight differences in detail will arise
from different computations from the same figures, and that a
study of the returns with no special knowledge gives the same
results as a compilation by a specialist at the time (the only
marked difference being for Cumberland, where the returns are
15s., 9s. to 15s., 12s. to 15s., which appears to show that 15s.
given by Villiers is too high for the average), and finally that
the divergence entirely disappears when we take the general
average.

For the next period, besides the returns, estimated in the
two columns on the principles just discussed, with averages
12s. 7d. and 12s. 8d., we have a great deal of evidence from the
Commission on Employment of Women and Children, summarized by Mr Little for the *Labour Commission* of 1894.

Passing over the intermediate years, the "*Richmond*" *Com-*
mission of 1880 gave Mr Druce and Mr Kebbel
materials for their summary : Mr Little made a
separate estimate, and in the few cases where he
differed from the others, published a figure intermediate between
his and theirs, from which I conclude that his estimate for
Surrey (e.g.) was 16s., since Mr Druce's of 15s. brings it down
to 15s. 6d. The original source of the two 1892 columns which
relate to weekly wages is one and the same, but Hasbach does
not make clear how he calculated his county averages.

The wage 10s. 6d. (for Gloucester in 1847) is entered to
emphasize the difference of wages for different
classes of labour : it is of course the case that

The Rich-
mond Com-
mission.

Summer and
winter wages.

shepherds, foremen, and horse-keepers are paid more than the general labourers, but it is not so obvious that ploughmen are; yet in many cases ploughmen's wages are given alongside those of general labourers, and are then 1s. 6d. or 2s. in excess. The figures throughout should refer to labourers not on piece-work, with no special skill or specialised work, and to wages that can be earned on an average throughout the year (assuming that they are paid in bad weather as well as fine) without allowing for extra money at hay or harvest-time. Wages are generally different in summer and winter, the two rates each prevailing 4 to 6 months. When both are given in a statement the average is of course taken; but difficulty arises when the statement is simply subdivided as 'ordinary pay,' 'hay' and 'harvest.'

The figures in the table are averaged for the years in which information is most complete, primarily to give a preliminary idea of the course of wages; but these averages must not be taken as the final statement which arises from the figures, if only because Wales has only been given the weight of a single county. The averages for separate districts are also given, and it will be seen that the rates of increase vary materially. The greatest increase is found in the northern group of counties, where the wages appear to have trebled between 1770 and 1890. It will be seen that the greater part of this increase was in the early part of the century; the explanation is that in the neighbourhood of the manufacturing towns and of the coal mines it was impossible to persuade the agricultural labourer to work for so much less than was paid for hardly more arduous work in mines and manufactures, as was possible in the more distant southern counties. On looking at the table at end of the book it will be seen that in the year 1880 two figures are given for Leicester, Rutland, and Notts: the higher figure is the wage paid in the part of the county near the mines, the lower in the other part of the county. This emphasizes the facts that the neighbourhood of other industries influences the rate of wages (so that, for instance, the rate in Middlesex can seldom be given at all accurately, and the rates in Kent and Surrey vary much from district to district), and that a county is

Averaging and comparison.

not a good unit over which to take an average; the proper unit would be a district in which the conditions of work were similar throughout. In making our general comparison this fact causes considerable difficulty, for whereas in the earlier commissions and inquiries a rough average was given for the whole county, in the report of the *Labour Commission* of 1894 districts were chosen throughout the country, not necessarily one in each county, but so chosen that every type of agricultural work was illustrated. When the comparison is made the only way to compare county with county is to assume that the district chosen by the *Labour Commission* is typical of the whole county in which it lies ; we cannot, therefore, place any great reliance on the rates of change of the county averages, but when we come to group the counties together according to their geographical districts, and still more when we come to group all the counties of England together, the minor fluctuations due to the causes indicated tend to be eliminated in the general average. This will be especially seen by looking at the figures in the table at end, where it may be noticed that the same result is obtained by different observers calculating on different principles, though possibly from the same data.

The figures given in the table have been worked up in a different way in the *Statistical Journal*, Dec. 1898, for the purpose of obtaining "index-numbers" for wages. Here the figures are given in their rough form with no interpolation, and the actual wages will sometimes appear divergent in the two tables, since the sources of information and the methods of averaging are not always the same. The apparent discrepancies will illustrate the difficulties of obtaining exact estimates for separate counties, while the agreement of the averages will show that there is safety when a sufficient number of figures are obtained. In the tables on pp. 32, 33 are given miscellaneous wage-statements which will be of use in tracing the course of wages between the dates of general estimates, and which formed a great part of the raw material for the working of county "index-numbers" in the paper just mentioned. The changes year by year are further shown by three consecutive wage-lists relating to single districts and classes of labour, and therefore more strictly comparable year by year than the preceding miscellaneous figures, which are due to diverse authorities. Finally the few general estimates of average wages and earnings are tabulated; the earlier figures appear to be estimates based on Young's and Eden's writings, and are therefore from the same sources as the earlier columns in the main table. The whole forms a very good example of the nature of the data on which the history of the wages in a great industry may be built.

It is worth while to review briefly a few historical events which affected this class of labour in particular. The Napoleonic wars combined with bad seasons to raise the price of wheat with great fluctuations   *Historical Summary.* from 50s. in 1793–4 to 120s. in 1801; the price averaged nearly 90s. over the period 1795 to 1821, at which date the fall came. During this time the scale of payment was entirely disorganized. It was not possible for the labourer to subsist on the 8s. 6d. paid in 1793. In some districts a considerable rise took place; in many the wages were habitually supplemented out of the poor rate. Sometimes by adjustment of wages, sometimes by adaptation of relief, the receipts of the labourer were made just sufficient to support him and his family whatever its size and whatever the price of wheat. All figures, therefore, relating to this period, whose evil effects continued till the Amendment of the Poor Law in 1834, must be handled with great care; in fact they do little more than show what the condition of the labourer would have been but for relief; no average has, therefore, been attempted and few figures are given for the war period. The spread of Chartism in 1831, and the continual alteration of the duty on imported corn, had their influence both on nominal wages and on their real value till the Repeal of the Corn Laws in 1846, since which agricultural wages have not been subject to such violent fluctuations. The continuous fall in the price of wheat has affected farmers and landlords far more than labourers, whose wages have in general kept their level or improved, while the fall of price has been of the greatest benefit in cheapening their staple diet; these causes have been supplemented by the continual stream of migration to the towns, and the consequent scarcity in the supply of agricultural labour. In the seventies the general disturbance, commercial activity and rising prices which followed the Franco-Prussian war, the movement for higher wages penetrated even to the country. Under the influence of Joseph Arch the labourers were organized in many districts, and on p. 33 is given his statement of the result. There can be no doubt that a rise took place, but how general, at what date, and how great, are matters of conjecture. It is best to look at the result after a partial reaction, and it will be seen that the rise between 1870 and 1880 varied in different districts from 1s. to 3s., and averaged 1s. 6d.

Miscellaneous Statements for Intermediate Dates.

Figs. [1] to [39] refer to Notes and Authorities, p. 35. For SUSSEX, vide pp. 36, seq.

Year	Place	s.	d.	Year	Place	s.	d.
1796	Surrey	10	0[1]	1813	Linc.	12	0[27]
,,	Bucks.	9	6[1]	,,	S. Wales	§13	9[7]
,,	Essex	9	0[1]	Average 1800-13	Norfolk	12	4[4]
1797	York, E.	11	3[1]	,, 1800-20	,,	12	0[4]
1798	Devon	7	0[1]	1806-13	Cumberland	15	2[4]
1799	Lincoln	10	5[1]	1805-15	Stafford	13	0[7]
1801	Leicester	11	0[7]	1814	Kent	16	6[7]
,,	Derby	11	0[7]	1815	Warwick	15	0[9]
,,	Herts.	11	0[1]	,,	Cheshire	12	0[7]
1803	Suffolk	11	3[1]	,,	Cumberland	14	6[7]
1804	Norfolk	12	0[1]	1816	Warwick	9	6[9]
,,	Suffolk	9	1[1]	,,	Hunts.	12	0[9]
,,	Wilts.	8	6[1]	During war:	Lincoln	15	0[9]
,,	Essex	9	9[1]	,,	Notts.	15	0[9]
1805-6	Essex	14	4[1]	1812-17	Somerset	13	6[5]
1807	Salop	14	0[7]	1813-20	Wilts.	9	9[4]
1809	Oxford	10	6[1]	1818-22	Putney	15	0[5]
1811	Worcester	10	0[7]	1821	Kent	12	0[4]
,,	Notts.	15	0[7]	,,	Norfolk	10	6[4]
,,	York, N.	<21	0[7]	,,	Wilts.	8	6[4]
,,	Glamorgan	15	0[10]	,,	Glamorgan	9	6[4]
,,	Manchester	15	0[38]	1822	Lancs.	16	6[28]
1812	Kent	18	0[4]	,,	York, W.	10	0[7]
,,	Wilts.	+9	0[7]	,,	Dorset (winter)	5	9[5]
1813	York, W.	16	6[7]	,,	Linc. (winter)	9	0[5]
,,	Hunts.	15	0[9]	1823	Norfolk	8	0[39]

		s. d.			s. d.
1819–24	Beds.	9 0[5]	1843	Linc.	11 0[14]
1825	York, W.	12 0[7]	1844	Beds.	9 0[31]
1826	Lancs.	14 0[29]	,,	Suffolk	9 0[36]
,,	Notts.	12 0[29]	1845	Stafford	12 0[25]
1831	Devon	7 0[37]	1846	Pembroke	7 0[30]
,,	Somerset	7 0[37]	1847	Kent	12 9[15]
,,	Essex	10 6[37]	,,	Somerset	7 0[20]
1830–3	Surrey	11 0[7]	,,	Gloucester	§10 6[15]
1832	Beds.	9 6[13]	,,	Leicester	11 0[15]
1834–6	,,	8 0[13]	1849	Manchester	15 0[34]
1838–9	,,	9 0[13]	1852	Cambridge	8 0[48]
1839	Gloucester	7 0[35]	1850–2	Suffolk	8 6[25]
,,	Manchester	15 0[34]	1823–53	Wilts.	7 0[47]
1840	Monmouth	13 6[40]	1854	Suffolk	13 0[25]
1842	Derby	12 0[20]	1855	Beds.	8 0[20]
1843	Wilts.	9 0[14]	1857	Warwick	12 0[33]
,,	Dorset	11 0[14]	1859	Dorset	7 6[32]
,,	Devon	11 6[14]	,,	Manchester	15 0[34]

Figs. [5] to [48] refer to Notes and Authorities, p. 35.

Mr Arch's statement[23].

			s. d.		s. d.	
In Lincoln wages rose from			12 0	in 1872 to	17 3	in 1875
Wilts.	,,	,,	9 0	,,	12 6	,,
Warwick	,,	,,	11 0	,,	15 6	,,
Dorset	,,	,,	9 0	,,	13 0	,,
Norfolk	,,	,,	10 0	,,	13 6	,,

Consecutive Statements by single Authorities.

Cumberland[43]		Northumberland[45]			Surrey[20]	
			Foreman	Hind	(Limpsfield)	
	s. d.		s. d.	s. d.		s. d.
1794	8 0	1831	12 6	11 0	1818–9	14 0
1795	8 2	1835	12 6	10 6	1820	13 6
1796	8 4	1840	14 6	12 0	1821	12 0
1797	9 0	1845	14 6		1822	11 0
1798	10 0	1850	13 0	11 0	1823	10 0
1799	10 6	1855	16 0	14 0	1824	11 0
1800	11 0	1860	17 0	16 0	1825–9	12 0
1801	11 6	1865	18 0	15 0	1830	11 0
1802	11 9	1870	20 0	16 0	1831–4	12 0

Cumberland[43]		Northumberland[45]			Surrey[20]	
			Foreman	Hind	(Limpsfield)	
	s. d.		*s. d.*	*s. d.*		*s. d.*
1803	12 0	1875	24 0	24 0	1835–6	11 0
1804	13 6	1880	21 0	18 0	1837–8	12 0
1805	14 6				1839–43	13 0
1806	15 0				1844	12 0
1807–10	15 6				1845	11 0
1811	15 3				1846–7	12 0
1812	15 0				1848–52	10 0
1813	14 6				1853–4	12 0
1814	14 0				1855–7	13 0
1815	13 6				1858–9	12 0
1816	12 0				1860–7	13 0
1817	11 9					
1818	11 6					
1819	11 0					
1820	10 6					
1821	10 0					
1822	9 6					
1823	9 0					
1824	9 6					

Statements of General Averages for England.

Authorities 44 and 12.

1780–90	1795	1795–9	1800–8	1805	1813	1818	1823	1831	1838
s. d.	*s. d.*	*s. d.*	*s. d.*	*s. d.*	*s. d.*	*s. d.*	*s. d.*	*s. d.*	*s. d.*
8 0	8 11	9 0	11 0	11 5	14 6	12 0	10 0	11 0	10 0

Authority 28.

1742–52	1761–70	1780–90	1795–9	1800–8
s. d.	*s. d.*	*s. d.*	*s. d.*	*s. d.*
6 0	7 6	8 0	9 0	11 0

,, 43.

1790	1795	1796	1803	1808
s. d.	*s. d.*	*s. d.*	*s. d.*	*s. d.*
8 1	8 7½	8 11	11 5	14 6

,, 22. Averages for 1767–89   1790–1803   1804–10

	1767–89	1790–1803	1804–10
	s. d.	*s. d.*	*s. d.*
	6 3	8 4½	10 0

,, 46.

1780	1800	1810	1820	1830	1840
s. d.	*s. d.*	*s. d.*	*s. d.*	*s. d.*	*s. d.*
8 1	11 5	14 6	12 0	11 0	11 0

,, 41.

1878
s. d.
14 0

,, 42.

1835	1880
s. d.	*s. d.*
10 0	15 0

Annual Earnings.

1866	1870	1891
£ s.	£	£
33 16⁴⁵	37¹⁹	40¹⁹

Notes and Authorities.

+ Specially valuable perquisites in addition to wage stated.   ? Evidence doubtful.   < The wage stated is a maximum.   > The wage stated is a minimum.   † In 1775.   * Glamorgan. ‡ These columns are estimates of total earnings.   †† 13s. 6d. married, 8s. single.   § Ploughman. ¶ Counting Yorkshire as three counties.

For more complete titles, see Bibliography in APPENDIX.

1 Arthur Young.   2 Eden.   3 Davies, *Case of Labourers.*   4 1821 Commission.   5 Wages and Poor Rates Commission, 1824.   6 Poor Law Commissioners, 1833.   7 Committee on Agriculture, 1833.   8 Poor Law Commissioners, 1834.   9 Agricultural Distress, 1836.   10 Lords' Committee, 1837.   11 Purdy, *Stat. Journal,* 1861.   12 Hand-Loom Weavers, 1839.   13 Poor Law Amendment, 1837.   14 Women and Children, 1843.   15 Agricultural Customs, 1847. 16 Caird, *English Agriculture.*   17 Returns of Wages, 1830—1886, and Returns of Agricultural Wages, 1860—1 and 1869.   18 Hasbach, Villiers and Purdy.   19 Little, in Labour Commission, 1893.   20 Women and Children, 1867—9.   21 Kebbel and Druce.   22 Hasbach.   23 Brassey, *Lectures on the Labour Question.*   24 Ed. Young, *Labour in Europe and America.*   25 "Richmond" Commission, 1880—1.   26 The Beehive, 1872.   27 *Labourers' Union Chronicle,* 1877. 28 Slaney, *Employment of the Poor,* 1822.   29 Commission on Emigration, 1827.   30 Operation of Mines' Act, 1846.   31 Agricultural Returns relating to Beds., 1844.   32 *Stat. Journal,* 1859.   33 Sargant, *Economy of the Working Classes.*   34 Chadwick, *Stat. Journal,* 1860. 35 Symons, *Arts and Artisans.*   36 *Times,* June, 1844.   37 Commission on Silk, 1832. 38 Weavers' Petition, 1811.   39 Brereton, *Agricultural Labourers,* 1824.   40 *Stat. Journal,* 1840. 41 Caird, *The Landed Interest.*   42 Mulhall, *Dict. of Statistics.*   43 Rooke, *National Wealth,* 1824. 44 Barton, *The Condition of the Labouring Classes,* 1817.   45 Levi, *Wages and Earnings,* 1867 and 1885.   46 Tuckett, *Labouring Population,* 1846.   47 *The Labourer's Friend.* 48 Commission on Depression, 1886.

SECTION V.

AGRICULTURAL WAGES IN SUSSEX : WAGES CONTRASTED
WITH EARNINGS.

DETAILS of the information with regard to a single county
throughout the period will illustrate well the
special difficulties that may appear, and show
how a very careful investigation might give the
solution of all the problems which arise, and result in a sequence
of wages almost year by year throughout the century. The
instance selected is Sussex, chiefly because certain preliminary
difficulties presented themselves in connection with
early years. In 1767—1770 Hasbach and Caird
quote Young and agree in giving the average as 8s. 6d.; in
1793[1] Young gives as the general county average
1s. 5d. per day in the winter, 1s. 9d. per day in
the summer, 2s. 4¾d. at harvest-time, and adds that piece-work
at harvest-time was paid at 8s. 5½d. an acre, from which we
deduce that on an average a labourer would reap an acre
in 3½ days. The details which he gives and on which presumably he bases his calculation are as follows[2]: daily wages at
Cuckfield, winter 1s. 4d., summer 1s. 6d., harvest £4 per
month; at Hunsey, winter 1s. 6d., summer 2s., while many
piece-prices are stated; at Eastbourne, winter 1s. 6d., summer

*Details of
wages paid in
Sussex.*

1770.

*1793: different
villages.*

---

[1] *General View of the Agriculture of the County of Sussex*, 1793.
[2] *Annals of Agriculture*, Vols. XXII.—XXIV.

1s. 9d., harvest 2s. 6d. first month, 2s. afterwards; at West Ham
and Pevensey, winter 1s. 6d., summer 2s., harvest 2s. 6d. for
wagoners, 3s. for reapers; at Battle, winter 1s. 4d., summer
1s. 6d., harvest 2s. and beer; at Beauport, winter 1s. 6d., summer
2s. to 2s. 6d., harvest 3s.; at Winchelsea, winter 1s. 6d., summer
2s., harvest 10s. 6d. to 11s. an acre, which a good labourer is
said to reap in three days, though as we have seen the average
is lower; at Salehurst, winter 9s., summer 10s., harvest 12s. per
week, reaping 8s. 6d. per acre; at Applesham, winter 1s. 6d.,
summer 2s., yearly earnings are given as £30, perhaps made up
as follows: 6 months at 9s. per week, £11. 14s.; 5 months at
12s., £13. 4s.; one month at 18s., £3. 12s.; total £28. 10s.,
which clearly leaves some extras to be accounted for; at Selsea,
1s. 4d. per day throughout, for 4 weeks at harvest-time £2. 15s.
and board, while on piece-work a man could earn 9s., 10s., or
11s. per week. Piece-prices for threshing, reaping, and mowing
are also very generally given throughout the county. From
this we deduce an average wage of 1s. 7d. a day, 9s. 6d. a week,
excluding harvest.

In February, 1795, the Eastbourne Guardians stated there
had been a rise in wages for weekly labour from   1795: Young
7s. to 8s. Young, in February, 1795, gives a wage   and Eden.
of 1s. 4d. or 1s. 6d. a day near Arundel; in December, 1795, at
Glynd[1] the wage was 1s. 6d. to 2s., at harvest it had been 2s.
to 2s. 6d., while a strong man on piece-work could earn 2s. to
2s. 6d. in the winter, and 2s. 6d. to 3s. in the summer. Eden[2]
states that in January, 1795, at Peasmarsh, the wage was 1s. 6d.
to 1s. 8d. in the winter, 2s. at hay harvest, and 2s. 6d. at corn
harvest, which was usually paid by the piece. At the same
date, at Winchelsea, 1s. 6d. was paid in the winter, 2s. for hay
harvest, and 2s. 6d. for corn harvest; in June, 1796, at Chailey,
1s. 6d. in the winter, 2s. in the summer. From
this it is seen that the weight of evidence is   Inconsistency
against the wage stated by the Eastbourne Guar-   of statements
    re Eastbourne.
dians, which is lower than any other wage given before or after

---

[1] The sequence on p. 38 refers to the same village; the daily wage there
given is 1s. 6d. in 1795, 2s. in 1796.

[2] *The State of the Poor*, Vol. III.

that date; so that we must think that either it is wrongly quoted or else refers to specially unskilled labour, and almost certainly to winter prices, in which season the statement was made. All the other evidence is consistent with a general rise of 1s. a week in 1794 or 1795, making 10s. 6d. as the normal wage.

The report of the *Commission on Depression*, 1821, states that in 1813 a married man with one child earned 13s., with two children 14s.; in 1821 with one child 9s., two children 10s. Slaney on the other hand gives 7s. to 9s. for 1822, his maximum being therefore the Commissioners' minimum. To reconcile all these statements we have the following list[1] showing a rise in 1794–6 and fall in 1821.

1813 and 1821.

1791–4	1795	1796–1800	1801–3	1804
9s.	10s.	12s.	13s. 6d.	12s.

1805–21	1822–33	1834–37	1838–40
13s.	12s.	10s.	12s.

A Select Committee of 1836 throws further light on these partially conflicting statements; there we find that the minimum or normal wage is 10s., while some earn 13s. or 14s. and even 16s., summer and winter, and that during the war the wage had been 12s. to 15s. Returning to 1824, the *Select Committee on Labour* gives wages in different places as follows: 9s. to 10s., 9s. to 10s., 9s. to 10s., 8s. to 10s., 9s. to 10s. 6d., 10s., 10s. 6d., 9s., 8s., 10s. 6d., showing an average 9s. 6d. In another place a witness says the wage was 9s. for married men, 6s. for bachelors. A letter of the Poor Law Commissioners[2] of 1833 gives 10s. as the maximum wage of 1832. The 1833 *Commission on Agriculture* states the wage from 1830 to 1833 as 10s. to 12s.,

1824.

1833.

---

[1] *Committee on Petition on Depression of Agriculture*, IX. of 1821 up to that date. Also published by Bischoff in *History of the Woollen Manufacture in 1842*, with the continuation, which may possibly not be comparable. Bischoff gives 10s. in 1795, while the Committee find no rise in that year.

[2] *Parl. Papers*, XXXII. of 1833, p. 317.

in 1833 as 8s. to 9s.; while another witness states vaguely that
the wage is from 9s. or 10s. to 12s. Reference is there made to
the *Commission on Emigration* of 1827, where a
complete statement is given as follows: man's   1827.
wage 10s. a week for 46 weeks or £23 a year, wife £5. 4s.,
parish £5. 12s., special payments for harvest and hay £6. 6s.
The Reports of the Poor Law Commissioners in 1834 show the
net annual earnings of a labourer, valuing all perquisites, was
about £33, while his ordinary wage if paid regularly through
the year would yield £32.

The list 1791—1840, given above, refers to only a single
farm at Glynde, near Lewes, at least before 1821. There the
fall after the war, beginning in general about 1818, may have
been delayed, or more probably the 12s. is carelessly given for
the whole 11 years, or else the wages at the place were simply
above the general average; further investigation might make
this clearer. In this connection we may notice
the statement in the *Labourers' Friend*, a news-   1818—1840.
paper of the forties and fifties, that in Sussex wages rose in
1830 from 8s. or 10s. to 12s. in 1831, under the influence of
Chartism, and rapidly fell again; and that in 1840 the average
was not more than 10s., married men being paid more than
single. Notice that the lowness of wages from 1834 to 1837 is
in agreement with the low general average of the country at
that time. The next figure is 10s. 6d. for 1851,   1857, 1860,
given by Caird; the returns of 1860 and 1870 call   1870.
for no special comment, and there appears to be no means of
filling in the gaps between these dates, in fact the only other
special statement is from Kebbel's *Agricultural Labourer*, that
wages in Sussex generally were, at the end of 1886, 2s., 1s. 9d.
or 1s. 6d. daily, and in East Sussex 12s. a week,
while annual earnings were £40. 4s.; and that the   1885—1888.
daily wage had been lowered 3d. in 1885 and 3d. in 1886, being
12s. after the second reduction.

Summarizing the results for this county, the following pro-
positions must be admitted as probable—that
wages in Sussex increased between 1770 and the   Summary.
height of the war scarcity in 1813 about 50 per cent., that they

then fell about 30 per cent. back to the level of 1793, and then rose slowly to their former maximum—that of 1813—in the seventies, since which they have fallen, but not far.

It is absolutely necessary to notice that these figures give Purchasing power. quite a distorted view of the labourers' condition, because of the change in the purchasing power of wages, and in fact that they only show half the factors of the problem, but to avoid stopping here to discuss the question of real and nominal wages, the labourers' weekly wages have merely been translated into pecks of wheat at the market price for the corresponding year; this method is very rough, since the years for which wages are stated do not necessarily correspond exactly with the date given for the price of wheat (which is a very fluctuating quantity year by year), the general price does not fluctuate exactly with the retail price in Sussex, and the price of wheat is of course not the only thing which decides the purchasing power of the labourers' wages. This correction is made only for Sussex, while the general average is left untouched, to indicate its necessity without attempting a definite statement for the whole country.

Weekly wages of agricultural labourers in Sussex.

	1767—1770	1793	1795	1813
Wages	8s. 6d.	9s. 6d.	10s. 6d.	13s.
Pecks of Wheat purchasable	5·7	6	4·5	4

	1821	1822	1824	1827
Wages	9s.	8s.	9s. 6d.	10s.
Pecks of Wheat purchasable	5	5·6	4·7	5·4

	1830	1831	1833	1834
Wages	11s.	12s.	10s.	10s.
Pecks of Wheat purchasable	5·5	5·8	6	7

	1836	1840	1851	1860	1870
Wages	10s.	10s.	10s. 6d.	11s. 7d.	12s. 2d.
Pecks of Wheat purchasable	6·6	4·8	9	7	8·3

	1872	1880	1885	1887	1892
Wages	13s. 4d.	13s. 6d.	13s. 6d.	12s.	12s.
Pecks of Wheat purchasable	7·3	10	13	12	12·7

It is clear that the weekly wage does not represent even the ordinary labourer's complete earnings, and a distinction is very generally drawn between weekly wages and annual earnings. In the first place extra wages are always paid at harvest time, often at hay-time; in the second place, many men earn additional money by occasional piece-work, which quantity varies from man to man and district to district; and in the third place, almost all labourers receive some perquisites. It would be almost possible to reckon all the additional receipts for harvest throughout the century if a special investigation were devoted to it, for in lists of wages a statement of the customary pay at harvest is very generally made. There are, however, more difficulties involved than at first sight appear, for the price is very often a piece-price, and as already noticed one man will reap an acre in three days while another takes four; the rates paid to the ordinary farm hands engaged throughout the year and to travelling gangs hired for the harvest are often different, while it is not generally possible to find from the lists given to which set of men the wage applies; and though the average duration of the harvest is also uncertain, we are sometimes told simply that the wage for the harvest month is merely a certain rate per day. The weekly wage is, however, a definite quantity, and when we are comparing one man's statement with another's on this subject we may generally expect that we are dealing with like quantities. The question of perquisites is even more difficult; statements often do not make clear whether the cottage is allowed rent-free; the question of the allowance for drink has already been discussed; the granting of free haulage of coals by the farmer, the allowance of a potato patch, the free keep of a cow, the daily pint of milk, wheat at less than market prices, and many other small items are generally considered too insignificant to mention except in the case of a very careful general estimate. There have been very few estimates of average earnings extending to the whole country; Levi in his wage census of 1866 states £33. 16s. as his estimate for the agricultural labourers' annual earnings, allowing apparently for

all perquisites and deductions; but the most important of
these estimates is that published by Mr Little in the *Labour
Commission*, to which reference has already been made, where
an account is given county by county both for the year before
the Commission—1892—and for a previous date, that of the
1870 Commission on the Employment of Women and Children;
these estimates are given in the table of "Weekly Wages of
Agricultural Labourers" at the end of the book.   His method is
to value with the utmost care every addition in the way of piece-
work or harvest payments and every perquisite or allowance, to
add the valuation of all this to the sum total of weekly wages
for the year and dividing the result by 52 to get a corrected
average weekly wage.   It will be seen on looking down the
list[1] that the difference between these earnings and wages
varies a good deal both from county to county and from year to
year, but we have the very significant fact that the difference

*Slow change
in the differ-
ence between
wages and
earnings;
Mr Little's
estimate.*

in the averages for the whole country is 2*s.* at
both the dates taken.   Now if it were always the
case that these additional earnings remained the
same in the same districts, it would not matter
in the least that we had only been able to make
the calculation for Mr Little's dates, and the slight average
difference that he finds in these earnings indicates that we
may make this supposition without great error.   A further
reason in favour of such an assumption is that the practice of
special forms of payment continues very rigidly in the same
districts generation after generation, so that a man may be
expected to add the same amount to his wages in decade after
decade; thus for short periods at least we may rely on the con-
servatism of the rural districts for obtaining accuracy in this
calculation; but on the other hand there has been a distinct
tendency throughout the century to substitute payment in
money for payment in kind, of whose effect there are no means
of making any exact estimate.   Leaving out of the question
the fact that labourers now very seldom board at farmhouses
(because for a perquisite of such value as this, allowance was
always made) we still have the substitution of money for drink,

---

[1] The columns for 1867—70 and 1892 in thick type give 'earnings.'

the removal of such favours as cheap corn, and the exaction of rent for cottages and ground more nearly at market price. It is clear that so far as this change has taken place, it tends to lower the rate of increase of wages shown in the table, it is hardly possible to say precisely to what extent: yet perhaps a limit to the change can be suggested, for a cottage in the early parts of the century would seldom be valued at more than 1s. a week, drink at hardly that amount; the whole difference now shown by Mr Little is only 2s. a week, and harvest earnings have perhaps increased rather than decreased. To put forward a tentative opinion, we may expect that the utmost addition to wages in the earlier periods which ought not to be made to make them correspond with later wages is 2s., while it is probably a good deal less[1].

Conclusion.

The information relating to annual earnings in Sussex is as follows:—Young's figures in 1770 indicate 8s. 6d. a week as the annual average; in 1795[2], 12s. will be near the mark; as we have seen £33 a year, equivalent to 12s. 8d. the week, was the estimate in 1833; Mr Little's estimate is 16s. 6d. in 1867—70, and 15s. in 1892, Mr Kebbel's 15s. 6d. in 1886.

It will doubtless seem that a good deal of this estimate for wages, in Sussex in particular and for the whole country in general, is not very far removed from guess-work, and indeed much of it is only approximate. In very many cases, however, we find that two different observers agree in their estimates, which fact places both on very much safer ground; we also find that directly we proceed to an average differences tend to disappear, that upward and downward tendencies have synchronised in the various districts throughout the country, and further investigation would very often remove the difficulties which remain. The object of this chapter is more to show the exact nature of the material at our disposal than to obtain any

Want of precision in these figures.

----

[1] For further discussion on this point, *vide Statistical Journal*, Sept. 1899, p. 556. The conclusion there reached is that the percentage difference between wages and earnings, when wages are averaged on certain principles, has on the whole varied very little.

[2] From Young and Davies.

very perfect or exact result, for I do not hold a brief for proving that wage statistics are sufficient to give a complete history of wages, but it is only my intention to examine what material does exist and how it can be handled. The further question, how accurate the result based on such material as this may be expected to be, should form the subject of a separate problem.

SECTION VI.

COURSE OF WAGES IN IRELAND[1].

BEFORE proceeding to the consideration of the various attempts at estimating the average wages for the United Kingdom, it may be worth while to illus- Wages in Ireland. trate the nature of the problem by examining the figures which relate to Ireland, and to notice in particular how much light may be thrown on the general course of wages even by scanty information. Statements of Irish wages are very deficient; even for agriculture they are Authorities: less frequent and complete than for England. Arthur Young gives figures for agriculture and artisans about 1777; a statistical account of the Irish counties Arthur Young. drawn up for the Dublin Society contains inter- Statistical Account. esting information relating to several districts at dates chiefly between 1801 and 1810; and as in the case of England, the agricultural labourer formed the subject of several enquiries between 1833 and 1840, completely summarized by Drummond[2], and the *Devon Commission on Occu-* Drummond. *pation of Land* carries on the figures to 1845; none of these contain many records of non-agricultural wages. Later we have the returns of agricultural wages throughout Great Britain and Ireland in 1861–62; special Poor Poor Law Reports. Law Inspectors' Reports in 1870 state wages in

---

[1] Cf. the article in the *Stat. Journal*, June, 1899, which is based on the same material.

[2] *Vide* Bibliography in APPENDIX.

all districts at that date, together with the percentage
Recent com-
missions.
increases since 1850; while since 1880 numerous
Commissions have furnished more or less inaccurate data. From all the official reports from 1870 to 1892,
such as those of the *Richmond Commission on Agricultural
Interests* 1879–82, the *Bessborough Commission on Landlord
and Tenant* of 1880–1, and the *Cowper Commission on the
Land Acts*, 1886, all information relating to agricultural wages
has been extracted by Mr Little in the Appendix to his Report
to the *Labour Commission*[1]. The Agricultural Sub-Commissioners of the *Labour Commission* also reported in great
detail on the condition of Ireland in 1892, but their statements
are unfortunately not summarized. Finally, detailed statements of current day wages are given in the Irish Agricultural
Statistics yearly since 1890. It will be seen then that we can
obtain general surveys in 1777, 1801, 1833–40, 1845, 1850,
1862, 1870, 1880, 1886, and 1890 onwards.

The difficulties that arise in the investigation of agricultural wages in Ireland differ in many ways from
Difficulties
of investiga-
tion.
those which we find when dealing with England
or Scotland. For England we had simply to find
the best method of averaging the reports from numerous
villages and then could proceed at once to a general view. For
Ireland, we have to deal with many different kinds
Methods of
payment.
of payment, too complicated to allow of a complete
discussion here, and with the great irregularity of
employment, which has varied immensely from district to
district and time to time. In the first half of the century it
appears to have been not uncommonly the case that certain
classes of labourers obtained only 100 days' work
Irregularity
of employ-
ment.
in the year, while they rarely made as much as 200
days' wages; this fact would have to be taken into
account before a complete estimate of the change of earnings
could be made, but unfortunately the materials for so doing do
not seem to exist. The day's rate also varies greatly in different seasons, and since the number of days in which the winter,

[1] *Labour Commission*, Vol. v. Part II. (C. 6894—XXIV.).

seed time, summer and harvest rates were earned varied greatly in different places, we should strictly compare annual earnings, not merely weekly or daily wages, as is generally sufficient in England. The only complete data for this comparison appear to be contained in Drummond's estimate for 1833–40; but in the reports of the *Labour Commission* of 1892 material is given for estimating total annual earnings.

Estimates for 1840 and 1892.

Annual Earnings.

	After Drummond		Labour Commission
	£ s.		£
Ulster	8 3	....	25
Leinster	5 10	....	25
Munster	4 10	....	28[1]
Connaught	3 10	....	23
Ireland	5 17	....	25

Both estimates apply to the class who may be regarded as the 'ordinary' labourer.

A less important difficulty is due to the fact that the Irish labourer not infrequently travels to England at the time of the English harvest, begging and borrowing on his way out, making in England or Scotland what are to him exceedingly good wages, and repaying his hosts on his way back: but it is hardly possible to take this into numerical account, and it is held to be a diminishing quantity now.

Migration.

There is great lack of information as to what perquisites or payments in kind have been common in Ireland: judging from the returns accessible it appears that when food is given the fact is generally stated, two meals a day being the ordinary allowance; their value is a matter of conjecture; a day's diet is reckoned as worth 4d. in Fermanagh in 1834[2], 6d. in Cork in 1860[3], and 6d. to 9d. in Antrim in 1894[4]. The

Perquisites.

Value of food.

---

[1] This figure is probably too high, but a study of the returns does not show any means of correcting it.

[2] Inglis.

[3] *Returns of Wages,* 1830 to 1886, p. 422.

[4] *Agric. Stat. of Ireland,* 1894.

question of providing drink is hardly ever mentioned. The
greater difficulty is the possession or hiring of land
by the labourer.   Mr W. P. O'Brien's evidence
before the Commission on the *Financial Relations
between Great Britain and Ireland*, 1895, throws
considerable light on this question; his evidence is the basis
of part of the following remarks.   Before the famine of 1846
there were three classes whose diet was chiefly potatoes: small
farmers, cottiers paying for two roods or an acre by labour
taken at a time when it would have been most profitable to
themselves, and labourers paying rent for land.   These last
were entirely dependent on their potato patch for support
during the four or six months they were out of work; the rent
was exacted at an exorbitant rate by the employers, who paid
themselves out of the wages earned by harvest labour the summer
after the land had been held.   Notice from this that the value
of land, when rented, cannot be fairly added to the wages
calculated on Drummond's method, since it was fully paid for;
but a considerable addition should be made for the value of the
labour spent on the patch to obtain the true annual income, an
addition of more proportionate importance than that of an
English labourer on his allotment.   In 1846 this
class received 6*d.* or 8*d.* daily, rising sometimes
to 10*d.* in the summer, but accepted even 4*d.* in the winter,
increasing their income by keeping pigs and fowls.   The ' *Devon* '
Commission of 1845 reported that their state was wretched in
the extreme.   It was on this poverty-stricken people that the
potato famine of 1845-7 came, with its results, the Government
system of relief, and the stream of emigration to
the United States.   By 1870, though the money
wages had greatly improved, there were still bitter complaints
on the part of the labourer that for a great part of the year he
could get no employment, and that he could no longer obtain any
land on whose produce he could subsist when wages failed.

By 1894 the condition had greatly improved.   In
Mr O'Brien's words, " Wages are higher, and what
is probably of more importance, employment is more constant,
owing to the great emigration which has taken place among

Land.

*Mr W. P.
O'Brien's
account.*

1846.

1870.

1894.

the class of able-bodied men. Their food is cheaper than it was
15 years ago, and their house accommodation (in Leinster and
Munster at all events) has undergone considerable improvement;
and carrying with them, as they do, those plots of ground, they
are enabled to keep pigs and fowls, to provide them with food
during the months they can get no employment." Diet is still
frequently given, representing more in value than the difference
between money wages where diet is and where it is
not free.   Since 1884 money wages have ranged   1884-1894.
from 9s. to 10s. without, 5s. to 6s. with diet; while 12s. without
diet, is paid near large towns; but the farmers cannot pay these
rates more than 6 or 8 months in the year, and though they
offer 8d. or 10d. a day, half the summer rate, the labourers will
not take it, for fear that the summer wage should come down
to the same price. None of these remarks apply to Ulster.

The only authentic list to hand of wages paid at the same
farm for a long period is given in the Irish Statistical Society's *Journal* for 1887, and will serve as   Wages near
a guide to the general change to be expected ; it   Limerick 1837-
refers to a farm near Limerick, and is as follows :   1885.

1837	1838–46	1847–54	1855–66	1867–70	1871	1872–85
1s.	1s. 2d.	1s. 4d.	1s. 6d.	1s. 8d.	1s. 10d.	2s.

The rise appears to have been nearly uniform and the
increase to have been 100 per cent. in 50 years.

It will now be clear that the statements of current wages
summarized in the following table must not be
taken as showing without further calculation the   Remaks on
rate of change of earnings; it rather shows the   figures tabu-
                                                    lated on p. 50.
average of summer and winter rates for a full week's work at
the various dates, and a difficult calculation is necessary for each
year to estimate the number of weeks worked annually, and the
additional value of perquisites or private labour. If we took the
figures from the reports of the *Labour Commission* with those
of the *Agricultural Statistics* of 1894, we should exaggerate
the real increase in 1893-4; for the figures for 1893 are the
results of the Assistant Commissioners' reports as to the
average weekly wages throughout the year, while those for

1894 are the simple average of such statements as the following :

Daily Wages	Summer	Winter
Ballyvaghan.. ......From 1s. 6d. to 2s. 3d.........From 1s. to 1s. 6d.		

These statements may include the harvest wage as the summer wage, and in that case in taking the average it would be assumed that this high wage was earned for three months instead of only one. A method which obviates this difficulty and makes the averages obtained from the Labour Commission Reports and from the Annual Agricultural Returns identical in 1893, is to assume that the average of the summer wages is paid for four and of the winter for eight months. The authorities for the various dates have already been stated.

Average weekly wages of agricultural labour[1],
(assuming 6 days' work a week).

	1756	1776–9	1801–10	1833–40	1850	1862
	s. d.	s. d.	s. d.	s. d.	s. d.	s. d.
Ulster		3 3	5 7	5 4	5 1	7 5
Munster		3 0	4 4	3 11	4 9	6 10
Leinster		4 1	5 3	4 6	4 11	7 2
Connaught ...		3 3	4 8	3 8	4 1	7 0
Ireland	2 6	3 6	5 1	4 6	4 10	7 2

	1870	1881	1886	1893	1894
	s. d.	s. d.	s. d.	s. d.	s. d.
Ulster	8 3	10 0	9 10	9 10	10 6
Munster	8 1	9 6	9 5	10 0	10 0
Leinster	7 5	9 0	9 5	9 5	10 6
Connaught	7 10	7 0	8 4	8 2	8 6
Ireland	7 10	9 0	9 4	9 5	10 0

The few scattered statements referring to the period 1800–1830 indicate that the wages in the war period were high, that a considerable fall followed the peace of 1815, and a compensating rise took place about the year 1830. In spite of the potato famine there appears to have been little change between 1840 and 1850, though 10d. per day was refused on the Government relief works in 1846. Comparing the general average with the list already given for

Intermediate dates.

---

[1] From *Statistical Journal*, loc. cit., except the column for 1894, which has been recalculated as explained in the text.

Limerick, it appears that the rates of increase are practically the same, except that in the latter the rise took place before 1850, instead of in the decade 1850–60.

In spite of the scanty records of artisans' wages in Ireland, a general idea of their rate of change can be obtained. The following tables contain the chief items of interest that have so far been found. *Artisans' wages. General view in comparison with England.*

Daily wages of Irish artisans and labourers compared with those in London, Edinburgh, and Glasgow at various dates.

	1776–9[1]					
	Masons		Carpenters			
	s.	d.	s.	d.		
Ulster	2	0	2	2		
Munster	1	7	1	7		
Leinster	1	9	1	9		
Connaught...	1	9	1	8		
London	2	8	2	8		
Edinburgh ...			1	4		

Kilkenny:		s.	d.
Carpenters and Masons, 1790		1	8[2]
Edinburgh: Carpenters, 1792		1	7[2]
Glasgow: Masons, 1794		1	10[2]

	1801			
	Masons		Carpenters	
	s.	d.	s.	d.
Londonderry[2]				
Best.........	3	6	3	6
Inferior ...	2	5	2	5
Meath[2]	2	5	3	3
Kilkenny[2] ...	2	2	2	2
London	3	2	3	2 approx.
Edinburgh ...	3	0	3	0 approx.

	1811		1831	
	Masons		Masons	
	s.	d.	s.	d.
Roscommon[2]	2	8½	2	6
Belfast[2]	2	9		—
London	4	6	4	6
Glasgow	2	10	2	4
Edinburgh ...	2	10	2	10

	1845			
	Bricklayers		Labourers	
	s.	d.	s.	d.
Dublin[3] ...	4	2	1	6
London ...	5	0	3	4

	Bricklayers					
	1855–6		1857		1860	
	s.	d.	s.	d.	s.	d.
Belfast[4] ...	3	4	4	0	4	3
Cork[4]	4	0	4	0	4	0

1863			
Dublin[4]:		s.	d.
Mechanics		5	0
Labourers		1	8
London:			
Building artisans		5	6
Labourers		3	4
Glasgow[4]:			
Building artisans		4	6
,, labourers		2	10
Edinburgh[4]:			
Building artisans		4	6
,, labourers		3	6

[1] Arthur Young, *Tour in Ireland*, Vol. II.

[2] *Statistical Accounts of Irish Counties.*

[3] Kane, *Industrial Resources of Ireland*, 1845. Kane gives the London wages as 22s. and 14s. per week: the figures in the text are from Section XII. infra.

[4] *Returns of Wages*, 1830–1886.

	1821-2	1824-5	1828-30	1831-3
	s. d.	*s. d.*	*s. d.*	*s. d.*
Londonderry[1]: Masons.......... ..	3 4	3 2	2 10	2 8
,, Labourers........	1 8	1 6	1 6	1 4
London: Bricklayers' labourers	3 2	3 2	3 2	3 2

For authorities for London, Edinburgh, and Glasgow, vide Section XII. infra.

From these tables it appears that the wages of Irish town labourers have been, like those of agricultural labourers, considerably lower than the wages of men doing similar work in England or Scotland; but that artisans on the other hand have been as well paid in Ireland as in any English or Scotch towns other than London. This fact was brought out by Sir R. Giffen in his evidence before the *Commission on Financial Relations.* He gave a table, showing standard rates of wages in 1894, from which the following is an extract:

Weekly wages of artisans.

	Dublin	Belfast	Glasgow		Manchester	London
	s. d.	*s. d.*	*s. d.*	*s. d.*	*s. d.*	*s. d.*
Shipwrights	36 0	33 6	33 9—36 0			42 0
Engineers (turners) ...	32 0	33 0	30 4½		33 0	38 0
Pattern makers	34 0	33 0	33 9		38 0	40 6
Carpenters (summer) ...	34 0	34 10½	36 0[2]		36 10	39 7
Bricklayers, Masons, & Plasterers' labourers (Summer)		18 0			26 0	27 1

The explanations offered are that skilled labour being mobile, artisans would quickly emigrate to Glasgow or Liverpool if the wages there paid were higher than in Ireland, that the supply of skilled labour in Ireland is more limited than the demand, and that the work of the unskilled labourer in Ireland is actually worth less than the unskilled labourer of England.

Not only are the average wages in the textile industries in **Textile Industries.** Ireland lower than in England, but also the chief Irish textile trade (linen) is the worst remunerated of the three chief textile manufactures. The figures are,

[1] *Returns of Wages,* 1830—1886.

[2] Not stated by Sir R. Giffen.

Average wages of all employed ; 1886[4].

	Ireland	United Kingdom generally
	£ s.	£
Linen	21 10	25
Wool	21 0	35
Cotton..................	——	36

The following short table contains practically all the remaining information as regards Irish wages before recent dates that has come to light :

Weekly wages in linen and cotton manufactures.

Linen.	1776–1800	1810	1812	1823
	s. d.	s. d.	s. d.	s. d.
Fine weavers: hand, weekly...	8 6[1]	6 4[1]	7 6[1]	12 0
Coarse ,, ,, ,, ...	6s. to 7s.[1]			
Spinning: daily, women	3½[1]			

	1830	1838	1848[2] Belfast
	s. d.	s. d.	s. d.
Fine weavers: hand, weekly...	6 0[3]	8 0[1]	12 0
Coarse ,, ,, ,, ...		4 6[1]	8 0
Spinning: daily, women		3[3]	(wkly.) 20 0 man

Cotton[1].	1791	1800	1810	1820	1838
	s. d.	s. d.	s. d.	s. d.	s. d.
Belfast: weaver, hand ...	24 0	18 0	13 6	9 0	7 0
spinner, man ...					21 0

Belfast Linen, 1886, weekly[4]

	s. d.		s. d.
Men, average	23 0	Spinners, women	8 5
Weavers, women	9 5	All hands	10 0

From these scanty records a general idea of the course of Irish wages can be obtained, but the figures are not sufficiently numerous or definite to allow the calculation of a numerical measure of the change. A large field is thus left open for research, for which the main lines of procedure have been laid down in this rapid and partial survey.

[1] *Hand-Loom Weavers Commission*, 1840.
[2] Thornton, *Overpopulation and its Remedy*.
[3] *Commission on Irish Poor*, 1830.
[4] Wage Census.

SECTION VII.

SCOTCH AGRICULTURE.

WAGES in Scotch agriculture differ in so many respects from all other wages here discussed that it is worth while to offer a brief review of them. The sources of information are described and the results tabulated and averaged in the *Statistical Journal*, March 1899.

In Scotland three principal classes of labour are to be found. The unmarried farm hand, man or lad,

The farm-servant and bothy.

generally described as a farm servant, who is boarded and lodged by his employer, either as a "kitchen" hand, living with the family, or in a "bothy," where several live and eat together. In the latter case a fixed allowance of meat and milk is paid, and a woman does part of the necessary service. The money wage is now on an average about £13 half-yearly for a competent hand. Early in the century it was very small: an old account-book shows that, in Argyllshire, 35s. or 37s. was paid a farm servant from Whitsuntide to Martinmas 1815; and £1 and 1 pair of shoes or 5s. for a cowherd, March 16 to Martinmas in 1816. In 1790 the average appears to have been £3 half-yearly. Estimation of the value of the board and lodging is rarely attempted; it was valued in Banff at £11. 5s. 0d. in 1869–70; in Aberdeen in 1890 board £8, cooking and fire £4, lodging £2. It is hardly possible to work out the change in earnings from the data, but it is important to notice that no safe comparisons can be made from the mere statements of these half-yearly wages, which are very frequently given.

Estimates should generally be based on the wages of another class : the married ploughman is the typical agriculturist. He has always been paid partly in cash and partly in kind, the chief exceptions being in Berwickshire, where payment was by a "boll," here meaning a fixed allowance of meal and milk and grain of various kinds, which was more than sufficient for maintenance, so that the surplus could be sold. In addition the labourers had a free house and garden and grass for a cow. In recent years cash has replaced kind, but not entirely; for in the absence of near markets the labourer is dependant on the farmer for haulage of coal and other necessaries, and it is an advantage to him if the farmer contracts to supply them. Many very careful estimates have been made at various dates as to the cash value of all these perquisites, and fair agreement is attained by different writers, but the necessity of this valuation diminishes the precision of the averages and comparisons which may be drawn from the figures.

The married ploughman, payment in money and in kind.

Here is a statement of the value of such a contract from the Labour Commission[1]:

Ross.   Engagements of Farm Servants, Whitsuntide 1891 to Whitsuntide 1892.

	£	s.	d.
Foreman ploughman. Money wages	26	0	0
Oatmeal delivered, 8 bolls[2] at 18s.	7	4	0
Potatoes 3 bolls, and 80 yds. drill	3	0	0
Coals 3 tons at 26s. delivered	3	18	0
Milk ¾ Scotch pint[3], summer 6 months ⎰ ...... „ ½ „ „ winter „ ⎱	3	0	0
Two loads firewood..................................		10	0
Fowls, value..	1	0	0
House rent-free	6	0	0
Total...	£50	12	0

When the house was not rent-free it was not at all unusual for the labourer to contract to supply a 'bondager,' frequently his wife, to furnish extra labour when needed at harvest; and it was often reckoned that the labour paid the rent. The net

---

[1] C. —6894, xv. p. 46.

[2] A boll is a Scotch measure = 8 stone.

[3] A Scotch pint = ½ gallon English measure.

cash value of the married labourer's earnings appears to have risen from £15 in 1794 to £49 in 1892, a wage which compares favourably with the £40 calculated for England.

The third class corresponds fairly closely to the day labourers whose wages are generally stated in the case of Ireland. They are not attached to the farm, as are the servants or the married ploughman, and do not generally have charge of horses. A difficulty in reckoning wages in this case arises from the fact that they depend on the length of the period for which the labourer is engaged, a point on which the returns are often not clear. If engaged by the day he will not obtain a full year's work, will make short hours or intermittent days in the winter, earn good wages in all busy times, and do very well at the harvest, a time when the attached labourer only adds his food to his other wages: on the other hand, he may be engaged week by week continuously through the year, when his weekly wages will be at a distinctly lower rate. In comparing the wages of this class, period by period, the same methods may be adopted as in the case of the ordinary English agricultural labourer; for though the total annual earnings made up by so many long and short days of ordinary work, so much piecework at thatching and ditching, and valuable perquisites at harvest, are difficult to estimate, yet when we compare the wages at two dates, it makes little difference to the ratio whether we simply average summer and winter rates at each date, or estimate so many days at each rate of pay. When the records are distinct this is simple enough, but the giving of meals in addition to money has been very frequent, indeed nearly universal at harvest-time, and we are often left in doubt whether their value is included in the wage; and even when it is expressly stated that food is additional the means are often lacking to determine its value. The result is that in the first place single statements are often valueless, and secondly that it is generally impossible to work out the changing ratios county by county, but it is necessary to average large districts to get a correct view of the change. When this is done it is found that the wages of unattached labourers have progressed step by step, and very nearly at the same rate, with those of the married ploughmen, and the few estimates extant of total earnings show that there is very little to choose between the earnings of the two classes.

The following table, abstracted from the *Statistical Journal*, shows the general trend of wages.

Wages in Scotch Agriculture.

1. Daily Wages of Day Labourers.

	1790	1794	1810	1834–45	1860	1867–70	1880–1	1890–2
	s. d.	s. d.	s. d.	s. d.	s. d.	s. d.	s. d.	s. d.
South Scotland...	1 0	1 2	1 9	1 7	2 3	2 5	2 10	3 0
North ,, ...	9	11	1 5	1 5	2 2	2 2	2 9	3 0
Scotland............	11	1 1	1 8	1 6	2 3	2 4	2 9	3 0

2. Estimated Annual Earnings of Married Ploughmen.

	1794	1810–13	1834–43	1867–70	1881	1892
	£ s.	£ s.	£ s.	£ s.	£ s.	£ s.
South Scotland ...	16 0	30 0	25 10	38 0	47 0	51 0
North ,, ...	13 10	25 10	23 10	33 0	42 0	45 10
Scotland............	15 0	28 0	25 0	36 0	45 0	49 0

3. Annual Wages of Unmarried Farm Servants, in addition to maintenance in kitchen or bothy.

	1790	1794	1804–14	1814	1834–45	1867–70	1892
	£ s.	£	£	£	£	£	£
South Scotland ...	7 0	8	17	14	12	22	27
North ,, ...	5 10	7	15	13	10	19	26
Scotland............	6 0	8	16	14	11	21	27

SECTION VIII.

GENERAL VIEW OF COURSE OF WAGES OBTAINED BY STUDY OF TWO OCCUPATIONS.

WE have seen that in the case of Ireland our only information, except for the most recent years, refers to agricultural labourers, building artisans, and to workers in textiles, but that we can get some idea of the progress and change in the rate of wages from considering only the wages in these staple industries. The trades of England and Scotland

Rough general view of course of English wages from consideration of bricklayers' and bricklayers' labourers' wages.
are, of course, very much more complex than those of Ireland, so that we cannot expect *à priori* to be able to obtain a result of any value from correspondingly few figures; but referring back to Section III. it will be remembered that if there is a general law of distribution of wages we can obtain considerable knowledge of the state of wages at any period, if we can find the position of only one or two points on the curve representing this law. If therefore we select two typical workmen and follow them throughout the century we obtain a result which will serve as an indication of the general course of wages. The workmen we choose must be those whose skill occupies a position whose relation to the skill of the whole working population has been unchanged throughout the century. We must not for instance take a spinner's wages, for at the beginning of the century spinning was done by a woman earning some 6*d.* a day, when her husband wove the yarn which she spun; but at the end of the century we should be dealing with one of the most highly skilled of modern workmen, surrounded

by the most complex and highly developed modern machinery, belonging to one of the best organised of trades and earning in good times one of the highest wages. Nor for similar reasons must we take the wages of a blacksmith who last century represented all the iron trades in one man, but whose successor we might look for with equal reason in a village smithy, in the Coventry bicycle factories and in Thornycroft's torpedo-works, making of course vastly different earnings. Perhaps the two best tradesmen to select, representing on the one hand un-skilled and on the other hand skilled labour, are those of the bricklayer and his labourer. The bricklayer makes very little use of machinery, his work is very much what it always has been, needing the same skill of hand and eye; his labourer is still a man whose business is simply to carry and place in the right position. Now if there has been no general tendency to increase or diminish the difficulty of work, or to increase the num-ber of unskilled who can obtain work at the expense of the number of the skilled, or vice versâ, then these two men will occupy the same position in the scale of wages now as at the beginning of the century. There is some reason to think that this supposition is not altogether arbitrary, for both then and now the bricklayer —then called 'mason' or bricklayer—earned much the same wages as the other tradesmen in the building trades, carpenters, plumbers, and so on, and is now inferior only to the best paid men in iron works, to coal-miners in the time of inflation, and to some others. Again, his labourer at the beginning of the century would not be differentiated from the ordinary labourer ready to turn his hand to any work from agriculture to porterage, and he obtains now also little more than the ordinary wages of unskilled labour in his district, though he will no longer work at any employment but his own. It will be possible perhaps to follow the wages of carpenters more easily than of bricklayers : we will therefore examine the information extant as to the wages of these three classes of men. In one of the MSS. in the Place collection it is stated that between the years 1777 and 1834 the wages of journeymen trades- men in London had undergone the following developments:— 1777, 18s. to 22s.; stationary or nearly so till 1793; raised by

1777—1834.
Francis Place.

Miscellaneous figures illustrating Changes of Wages.

Weekly wage of	1777	1793	1795	1802	1807	1810	1813	1815	1820	1823	1825	1830	1832	1834	1838	1840	1849	1859	1870	1880	1883	1884	1894
	s. d.	s. d.	s. d.	s. d.	s. d.	s. d.	s. d.	s. d.	s. d.	s. d.	s. d.	s. d.	s. d.	s. d.	s. d.	s. d.	s. d.	s. d.	s. d.	s. d.	s. d.	s. d.	s. d.
London Artisans, after Place to 1834[1]	18 0	22 0	25 0	27 0	30 0	33 0	36 0	36 0	36 0	36 0	36 0	36 0	36 0	36 0					35 0				38 0
Labourers																							26 0
Portsmouth Dockyard: Shipwrights		25 0	28 6	25 0	28 0	28 6	28 0	27 0	27 0	22 0													32 10
Labourers		11 0	14 6	13 0	14 0	14 6	14 0	14 0	10 0	11 0													
Generally in Provinces: Artisans			16 6												20 0								
Macclesfield: Artisans	18 0							24 0	24 0	24 0	24 0	24 0	24 0		22 0								33 0
Labourers	10 0							16 6	16 6	16 6	16 6	16 6	16 6		14 0								20 9
Bedfont, Middlesex: Labourers							18 0	15 0	12 0	12 0	12 0	12 0											
Manchester[2]: Carpenters		18 0			25 0	25 0	25 0	25 0	22 0	24 0	24 0		24 0	24 0	26 0	27 0	28 0	28 6	32 0	38 0	36 7	36 0	35 0
Bricklayers		18 0			22 6	22 6	22 6	22 6	21 6	24 0			18 6	23 6	27 0	28 0	28 0	31 6	32 6	43 0	38 7	36 0	38 0
Labourers		13 6			15 9	15 9	15 9	15 9	14 9	14 0	16 0		12 0	15 0	18 0	18 0	18 0	19 6	20 6	23 5	25 0		25 3
Mr Mulhall: Mason	17 0								25 0							23 0		30 0				35 0	29 0
Carpenter	15 0								20 0							20 0		25 0				30 0	25 0

(Portsmouth Dockyard Shipwrights 1894 column noted "1891"; Mr Mulhall 1894 column noted "1886".)

---

[1] *Vide* note 1 on page 61.   [2] *Vide Returns of Wages*, p. 38, for the years 1810–1825.

successive strikes to 25s. in 1795, 27s. in 1802, 33s. in 1810, and 36s. 1813, at which point they remained till 1834, the date of the MSS[1]. This development is stated to be typical not only of the trade to which the figures actually refer, but to a million working men. Another series of figures for this early period, not of bricklayers, nor carpenters, but of workmen of somewhat similar character are contained in the records of Portsmouth Dockyard; here we find that a shipwright earned on an average about 4s. at day-work from 1790 to 1793, 4s. 9d. from 1805 to 1810, 3s. 8d. in 1823; that labourers in the Dockyard throughout received almost exactly half the shipwright's wages, but that during the time of war, especially 1805–1815, their wages were increased immensely by undertaking piece-work at nearly 50 per cent. in excess of their time wages.

Shipwrights at Portsmouth 1793—1823.

Still, keeping to an early date we find that, according to Eden[2], in the provinces, in 1795, artisans earned from 2s. 6d. to 3s. per day, and we have seen that agricultural labourers earned at the same period about 1s. 6d. Going to another special district we find the following list from Macclesfield:—

Builders at Macclesfield, 1793—1838.

		s.	d.			s.	d.
1793	Artisans...	3	0	Labourers...		1	8
1815–32	„ ...	4	0	„	...	2	6 to 3s.
1838	„ ...	3	8	„	...	2	4

This is one of those valuable lists of wages given accidentally, as it were, in an Enquiry into the condition of other workpeople —in this case of the Hand-Loom Weavers, valuable because it is hardly possible that they could have been given with any bias. To take other special districts: in Middlesex, labourers[3] earned 3s. in 1811–13, 2s. 6d. in 1814–18, falling to 2s., and further to 1s. 8d. in 1822; 2s. in 1823–30. For Manchester we have the following four tables, besides much other information:—

Manchester building trades.

---

[1] The figures are of the wages of breeches-makers, which were higher than those in the building trades.

[2] Eden, *State of the Poor*, passim.

[3] Porter, *Progress of the Nation*.

Manchester : Building trades[1].

i.	1839		1849		1859	
	s.	d.	s.	d.	s.	d.
Bricklayers...............	27	0	28	6 [2]	31	6 [2]
„ Labourers...	18	0	18	0	19	6 [2]
Joiners	26	0	28	0	28	0

ii.	1834		1884	
	s.	d.	s.	d.
Bricklayers...............	23	0	36	0
Joiners	24	0	36	0

iii.	1832		1840		1846	
	s.	d.	s.	d.	s.	d.
Bricklayers.................	18	6	27	0	28	6
„ Labourers...	12	0	18	0	19	0
Carpenters.................	24	0	27	0	27	0

iv.	1850		1860		1870		1877		1883	
	s.	d.	s.	d.	s.	d.	s.	d.	s.	d.
Joiners	24	0	27	0	32	0	38	7	36	4
Bricklayers...............	26	0	30	0	32	0	43	0	38	7
„ Labourers...	17	0	18	0	20	5	23	10	25	0

We next find a statement in the *Beehive*, a newspaper of 1870, giving the wages recognised by trade unions throughout London, resulting in an average for a good tradesman of 35*s.*; in particular, bricklayers' men were paid at 8*d.* an hour, that is 6*s.* 8*d.* a day, and carpenters at very nearly the same rate. The *Labourers' Union Chronicle* of 1877 quotes from Sir J. Lowthian Bell that in the north of England in 1874 wages of carpenters were 5*s.*, and of brick-layers 5*s.* 6*d.* a day. With this should be compared the recog-nised rates in London and northern towns, which were in 1893 :

Miscellaneous.

Weekly Wages in 1893.

	Bricklayer[3]		Bricklayer's Labourer[3]	
	Summer	Winter	Summer	Winter
	s. d.	s. d.	s. d.	s. d.
Newcastle.........	37 6	33 0	25 0	23 6
London............	39 7	36 0	27 1	24 9
Macclesfield	34 1	32 4	21 7	20 1
Manchester	40 10	31 1	27 3	23 3

[1] i. Chadwick, *Stat. Journ.*, 1860. ii. Montgomery, *Manchester Stat. Soc.* iii. McCulloch's *Statistical Account of the British Empire.* iv. George Lord's evidence before the Commission on Depression of Trade, 1886.

[2] Average of summer and winter rates.

[3] *Report on Standard Time Rates*, 1893.

These figures will all be found to agree fairly well with Mr Mulhall's estimate in his *Dictionary of Statistics*, viz.,—

Mulhall's estimate.

		s.	d.			s.	d.
1780	Mason	17	0	Carpenter ...		15	0
1820	,, ...	25	0	,,	...	20	0
1840	,, ...	23	0	,,	...	20	0

With this compare Symon's *Arts and Artisans*, p. 3 :

1839 Mason 18s. to 22s.   Carpenter 20s. to 25s.   Bricklayer's labourer 12s.

Mr Mulhall's later figures are :—

		s.	d.			s.	d.
1860	Mason	30	0	Carpenter ...		25	0
1880	,, ...	35	0	,,	...	30	0
1886[1]	,, ...	29	0	,,	...	25	0

As regards the relation between the rate of change of wages in the building trades and the average rate of change for the industries of the United Kingdom in general, to quote from a paper already mentioned[2], it appears that from 1860 to 1877 wages in the building trades and the general rate increased 28 per cent., but from 1877 to 1891 in the building trades they remained stationary, but in other trades increased on an average 5 per cent.; on the other hand, in the last two or three years there has been a general movement in the building trades to increase wages $\frac{1}{2}d.$ to $1d.$ an hour, that is to say, 5 to 10 per cent., so that it is quite probable that by the present date, 1899, the level has been restored again. Thus the rate of change found in the building trades, as represented by the bricklayer, his labourer and the carpenter, throughout the century will serve as an indication of what we may expect when our investigation is complete.

---

[1] Mulhall, *Fifty Years of National Progress.*
[2] Statistical Society's *Journal*, June, 1895.

SECTION IX.

GENERAL ESTIMATES OF WAGES.

THE first general estimate available for our purpose is one given in Colquhoun's *Treatise on Indigence*, of which the following is an excerpt:

Colquhoun.

1803.

No. of persons	No. of heads of families	Description	Average yearly income	Aggregate income
			£	£
	446,000	Artisans	55	24·5 million
190,000	50,000	Soldiers....................	29	5·5 ,,
130,000	38,000	Navy.......................	38	4·9 ,,
180,000	67,000	Sailors	40	7·2 ,,
	340,000	Agricultural labourers	31	10·5 ,,
	40,000	{General labourers in mines, canals, etc. ...}	40	1·6 ,,

Average £43

This table is also given in Tuckett's *Past and Present State of the Labouring Population.* The next complete estimate is not till after 1860, but there are enough wages given at several dates to make an estimate of the total amount paid annually in wages possible, if difficult. In 1795 we find in Eden's and Young's writings enough wage statistics to make such an estimate possible, the chief difficulty being to know the numbers of labourers, the numbers of artisans, and the numbers which are paid at each separate wage.

Eden and Young.

Next we have in 1824 in the report of the *Commission on Artisans and Machinery,* and in the report of the Select Committee on the custom of paying labourers' wages out of the poor rates for the same

Material in Reports of Commissions 1824–1840.

year, material for finding the rate of wages in the most important industries. In the reports on agriculture from 1833 to 1840 together with the reports on hand-loom weavers in 1838–40, we again have enough information to enable us to form a very good idea of the wages for all different occupations, and by combining these with the census figures—which by this date are beginning to be of use for calculations of this nature—we could obtain an estimate which would perhaps be right within a small percentage.

In 1867 Dudley Baxter made a complete estimate of national income, from which the following are the relevant particulars:
Baxter.

England and Wales.

All earners	Number	Average	Total
		£ s.	£
Highly skilled labour and manufactures ...	1,123,000	50 0	56,149,000
Lower ,, ,, ,, ...	3,819,000	33 10	127,921,000
Agriculture and unskilled	2,843,000	24 10	70,659,000
	7,785,000		£254,729,000

Adult Males	£ s.	All employed	£ s.	
England and Wales	45 0	England and Wales	32 10	
		Scotland	28 5	together £30
		Ireland	19 0	

Total Income Manual Labour Class... £324,645,000.

To compare with these and carry us on another 20 years we have Leone Levi's two estimates for 1866 and 1885; these are the most thorough accounts up to those dates of the rates of wages for all occupations, and present very complete pictures of the condition of the working classes.
Leone Levi.

The results given for annual earnings of adult males are:

	1866		1884	
	Adult males	All workers	Adult males	All workers
	£ s.	£ s.	£ s.	£ s.
England	58 10	40 6		46 12
Scotland	53 6	36 6		41 6
Ireland	37 6	30 0		23 6
United Kingdom ...	50 0	37 10	56 0	42 14
Total	£418,000,000		£521,000,000	

Great as is the difference in the results of Baxter's and
Levi's enquiries as thus crudely stated, on comparison item by
item it is found that the differences arise much more from
questions of definition than of fact, except that Baxter estimates 10 and Levi 4 weeks as the average lost time during the
year. The weekly wages for all workers are:

Baxter, 1867	Levi, 1866
14s. 3d.	15s. 8d.

The next estimate which should be consulted is Sir Robert
Giffen's *Essay on Recent Accumulations of Capital*,
Giffen. where wages are not given, but the total of capital
and of resulting income can be compared with Baxter's and
Levi's estimates. These estimates however, Young's, Colquhoun's, Baxter's, and Levi's, are none of them more than
approximations; they do not profess to be a rigid account of
the annual earnings of labourers, but are merely the results of
very extensive enquiries made by the authors in person or by
deputy in all the districts in which important industries were
carried on. It is hardly possible that any one man should have
sufficient knowledge of the peculiar circumstances in each
industry, to be able to estimate from the somewhat vague
returns he would obtain the true annual income of the working
class in all employments.

The first real wage census, that is to say, an investigation
into the actual wages paid to all members of the
Wage Census. working class, was commenced in 1885 by the
Board of Trade; it was not exhaustive, because the method in
which it had to be carried out of necessity confined it to trades
located more or less in distinct centres, or at least carried on in
factories or by groups of organised men. Sir Robert Giffen
estimates that the figures which the Department collected
represent the actual condition of about three-quarters of the
whole number of the working classes, and thinks it not unlikely
that the averages are typical for a yet wider group. It would
be incorrect to speak of this investigation as being complete in
the same sense as the Population Census is, for all the returns

made to the Department were voluntary. The Department having made a preliminary investigation of the districts where certain trades were carried on, and having found the names of the chief firms engaged, drew up careful blank forms on which were to be stated the nominal weekly wages in a full working week paid to each class of workman, and the number of workmen receiving that wage. They further asked for the total wages paid in the previous year, and for the total wages and number employed in the busiest and slackest week of the previous year, by this means obtaining data for measuring the amount of want of employment which might be expected in each trade. Besides the wages stated for manufacturing districts and by large employers, many other figures are given in the reports of the census arising from returns of masters' or men's associations or unions.

A considerable portion of the persons addressed, some 25 to 35 per cent., neglected the request entirely or filled in the forms so badly as to make them useless, and it is possible that these particular firms were those   *Its defects.* which were in the habit of paying the worst wages. It is not likely, on the other hand, that the returns of the employers who met the requirements of the Department are at all far from the facts, so that we probably have an accurate account of the wages throughout all the important concentrated or well organised industries, except in the worst paid factories in those industries. No returns were made respecting shopkeepers' assistants, domestic servants, or workers in their own homes, such as tailors and dressmakers; so that again the worst paid persons are likely to be excluded from this census. Further, no account is taken of casual labourers who belong to no trade or to those who are chronically out of work, so that the census, though on a very large scale, still does not represent the whole sphere of industry. It will be found, however, that the area covered corresponds fairly closely with that covered previously by Leone Levi.

The general result of this census as compared   *Rough comparison.* with previous estimates may be briefly stated as follows :

United Kingdom.

	The Census 1886		Levi 1884	Estimates of Levi 1866	Baxter 1867
	weekly	annually (46 weeks)	48 weeks	48 weeks	42 weeks
	s. d.	£ s.	£ s.	£ s.	£ s.
Adult males ...	24 9	57 0	56 0	50 0	
Men, women, lads and girls	17 6	40 0	42 14	37 10	30 0

46 weeks is taken for the census estimate, since it appears from the information in the reports that 6 weeks is about the average lost time.

Though each of these estimates, from Colquhoun's in 1806 to the Board of Trade's in 1886, is probably fairly accurate in itself and complete as far as it goes, it is for many reasons not safe to take the average figures and say that the rate of change of these figures represents the rate of change of the average wage. There are very many difficulties in defining who should be rightly counted as manual workers, and probably the same definition was not employed by Colquhoun as by the Board of Trade or by intermediate workers. Different methods also may have been used for computing annual earnings from nominal wages; it is difficult even to lay down a definition of what do constitute annual earnings, and it is probable that even obvious constituents of these earnings, viz. daily or weekly wages, all payments in kind, free house-rent, and so forth, were not included in quite the same way by the different investigators; so that we may expect that not only each estimate is a certain percentage (it is difficult to say what) incorrect in itself, but that when we come to compare one of these estimates with the next, a further error of unknown magnitude will be included; so that for instance if Colquhoun's estimate was 10 per cent. in defect according to his idea of what he was reckoning, and the Board of Trade's 5 per cent. in excess of earnings according to their meaning, and further that the amount which should have been included in Colquhoun's estimate on his idea, represented a quantity 15 per cent. less than what the Board of Trade would have included if they had been estimating for that.

Difficulty of comparing these general estimates.

earlier date (all these figures are purely hypothetical), then the total error in the comparison of their estimates would have been the result of the combination of this 10 per cent., 5 per cent., and 15 per cent.; an apparent increase of say 50 per cent. would be in reality an increase of only 9 per cent.[1] It is probable that these figures are considerably in excess of the actual errors, but they serve to show that caution must be used in comparing the figures at the different dates. It is clear that the fault of all these comparisons comes from our being obliged to take the "statical" point of view, but if on the other hand we could compare wages of each class of workers for short periods, knowing that in each case they were estimated on the same methods, and then combine all these different rates into one average rate, we

Necessity of "kinetic" method.

should be rid of the greater of these errors. There are two ways of setting to work in this latter or "kinetic" method; we may either start at the earliest date possible, taking the wages which we can then find, work out the rates of increase for these persons period by period, and so come up to the present date, and make estimates as best we can for the effect of the introduction of new trades and new classes of workmen not represented in our primary figures; or we can adopt the reverse method, which will be found simpler for calculation, and starting in modern times, on the basis of the Board of Trade wage census, work backwards, and find the ratio of earlier wages to latter wages, letting each trade, as we come to its origin, automatically drop out of our calculation. An illustration of this process is given further on (*vide infra* p. 91 seq.).

Pending a more exhaustive tabulation of material on the "kinetic" method, it may be worth while to put together the wages which from our investigation so far appear to be typical

---

[1] Suppose that Colquhoun estimated £16, the Board of Trade £24; increase $50\,\%$. By hypothesis Colquhoun's estimate on his own assumptions should have been $£16 \times \dfrac{100}{90}$, and the Board of Trade under the same circumstances would have estimated $£16 \times \dfrac{100}{90} \times \dfrac{100}{100-15} = £20 \cdot 95$; at the same time the £24 should have been $£24 \times \dfrac{100}{105} = £22 \cdot 86$. Increase $£1 \cdot 91$, i.e. $9 \cdot 1\,\%$.

of large groups of workmen, and so obtain a general, if inaccurate, idea of the change of wages on the "statical" method. The following table appears to be consistent with itself and with the information coming from the better known sources and the calculations of general averages hitherto published, but it is purely tentative, and must not be quoted as if it were a result of exhaustive investigation.

Tentative table of Average Weekly Wages[1].

	1795	1807	1824	1833	1867	1897	Weights use in taking average
	s. d.	s. d.	s. d.	s. d.	s. d.	s. d.	
London type of artisan	25 0	30 0	30 0	23 0	36 0	40 0	1
Provincial ,,	17 0	22 0	24 0	22 0	27 0	34 0	2
Town labourers	12 0	14 0	16 0	14 0	20 0	25 0	3
Agricultural labourers .	9 0	13 0	9 6	10 6	14 0	16 0	3
Weighted average......	13 6	17 0	18 0	16 2	21 4	25 6	

Colquhoun, 1803	Levi, 1866[2]	1884	Wage Census, 1886
16s.	21s.	23s.	24s. 6d.

The weights applied are almost arbitrary, and of course greatly affect the result.

[1] Compiled independently of Mr Wood's figures given to the British Association, Sept. 1899, and published in the *Economic Journal*, Dec. 1899.

[2] Levi's estimate for 1879, of which I have only been able to find somewhat unsatisfactory quotations, appears to give the following average weekly wages for the United Kingdom:

	s.	d.
Adult males	21	3
All workers	16	6

Other evidence indicates that this estimate is too low.

SECTION X.

PRINTERS' WAGES.

THE wages of printers have a very complete record throughout the century, especially in London, Manchester,
Edinburgh, and Glasgow; in some cases we can
trace the rates of wages onwards from 1775.
Since 1845 also, thanks to the complete organisa-
tion of the printing trades, we are able to find the rates of
wages in many provincial towns and in Ireland. There is so much
material for this study that limits of time have prevented the
extraction of all the results which it is capable of yielding, but
the general course of wages is quite clear and may be described
in a word as one of slow but steady increase. Wages are paid
in a printing establishment on two entirely distinct bases: weekly time-wages to those who are
said to be on the "'stab," and piece-wages based
essentially on the number of letters printed. It will be necessary throughout to keep these two rates as distinct as if they
belonged to two different trades, though of course it will be
generally found that increases in the time and piece-rates have
taken place nearly simultaneously and that the proportionate
increments have been nearly equal. The introduction of the
measurement by the thousand ens, that is to say breadths of
letters equivalent to the letter n is said by Mr Sydney Webb
to date from 1774[1], and the rate given for ordinary print
(from brevier to english) for ordinary matter is the basis of the
piece-rates, so that if we know the number of pence per

Printers:—
Complete-
ness of wage
record.

Methods of
payment.

[1] *Vide, Labour in the Longest Reign,* p. 12.

thousand ens brevier we need, generally speaking, not trouble about any other piece-rates. As the type becomes smaller the piece-rate per thousand ens increases; as the work becomes more complicated by the introduction of footnotes, tables of figures, foreign words or the like, a further addition is made to the piece-rates. Parliamentary work in England and Session work in Edinburgh are also paid at increased rates, and when a piece-rate is given for daily newspapers that is also generally higher than the ordinary standard. The basis of the time-wage may similarly be taken as the time-rate paid for jobbing-work, book-work, or weekly newspapers; for bi- or tri-weekly papers the rate is higher, presumably because the work is done at higher pressure; for evening daily papers it is higher again, the highest of all being naturally for morning papers, where the work is done very rapidly between 9 p.m. and 2 a.m. Since the ratio of one of these rates to the other does not change much it will not be necessary, for a preliminary survey, to pay attention to more than one of them, though in considering the average wages in the trade the steady increase of newspaper as compared with book matter should of course be taken into account.

Wages of Printers' Compositors, London.

	Price per 1000 (brevier)	Time wages	Morning News	Evening News
	d.	*s. d.*	*s. d.*	*s. d.*
1785	4½	24 0	27 0	
1786			31 6	
1793		30 0	36 0	34 0
1800	5¼		40 0	37 0
1805		33 0		
1809			42 0	39 0
1810	6	36 0	48 0	43 6
1816	6[2]	33 0	48 0[1]	43 6[1]
	unchanged to 1847	reduction brought about gradually in 2 or 3 years	never yet changed	never yet changed

[1] Very few are paid in this way in London, and numbers on "'stab" on morning newspapers have diminished.

[2] Reprints after 1816 were paid at ¾d. less than new work.

During the stationary period 1816–47 slight alterations
were made in the more complicated price-lists corresponding
with changes in the nature of the matter printed. It should
perhaps be explained that these high wages do not apply to
everybody employed since there are supernumeraries on the
papers at one half these wages throughout. Another statement of the wages from the London Society of Compositors
gives rates which differ slightly from, but show an almost
identical rate of increase with those given above, which are
taken from the official table of the London Scale of Prices, the
revised list being dated 1835. There was a partial reduction
in 1816 of time-wages, but the next list we find
shows that they were at 33s. from 1846–65, at 36s.   1846—1899.
from 1866–90, and at 38s. from 1891–99. The price for
"brevier" remained at 6d. per thousand for new work till 1866,
when a rise of ½d. took place; further rises of ½d. in 1872 and
1891 brought the rate to 7½d., at which it stands in 1899.

Turning now to Edinburgh our record begins with the
dispute in 1804, which is remarkable in very many
respects. The Edinburgh printers claimed that   Edinburgh
                                                        dispute in 1804.
their rate of pay had always been 1d. per thousand
less than the London scale, but that they had not received the
increase which we have just seen was obtained in London in
1800; they further stated that their time-wages were very low,
and claimed an increase. They drew up a list of wages paid at
the printing houses where the "session" work was done both
in time and vacation, and in ordinary "book-houses," which
appears to show that the average amount received was about
14s. 6¼d. in 1773, 19s. 8¼d. in 1791, and 18s. 5d. in 1802. The
masters on the other hand drew up a list showing a much
higher rate of pay. The printers claimed to have their wages
officially arranged, and this is one of the most interesting and
celebrated instances of such an appeal having been made;
another is recorded, also for Scotland, in connection with the
hand-loom weavers, their appeal being in 1810. The varying
statements of the men and masters were submitted to an
accountant, who came to the conclusion that the
wages of the whole trade had been very nearly as   1773—1804.

the men stated, in fact 14s. 6d. in 1773, 19s. 8d. in 1791, 18s. 5d. in 1802. It was therefore decided that a clear case had been made out for an increase, and the decision was that for ordinary printing, that is to say brevier, the rate was to be raised to 4½d., making 20s. about the average amount to be obtained in the week. Regular time-work was apparently infrequent at this date, but the records are not clear. For the next 40 years the changes in piece-wages appear to have followed very closely

1804—1891.

those in London, and it will be sufficient to state that in Edinburgh from 1880 onwards the rate has been 6½d. per thousand. For time-wages we very soon find records of the rates paid in the capital and provinces, published year after year, as by the Scottish Typographical

General rates in Scotland.

Society; the lists are singularly complete, so that it will be possible to work out year by year an average for all members of the trade who belong to any Society, but we can obtain a very good idea of the rate of wages without going through this labour. The plan adopted is to watch the changes in Glasgow and Edinburgh, the best paid towns in Scotland, to also take a town half-way down the list, the "median" town we may call it, and further to choose one or two towns which have remained throughout at the bottom of the scale; the relative order has not changed much during the period.

We have then the following table:—

Weekly Time-wages of Compositors[1].

	1791	1805	1833	1839	1844
	s. d. s. d.	s. d.	s. d.	s. d.	s. d.
Glasgow	10 6 to 18 0			25 0	25 0
Edinburgh		25 0	21 0[2]		23 0
Percentage of 1891 wage......		79	66	......	73

[1] Some of these figures are from the Webb MSS. ; that for Glasgow, 1791, is from the *Stat. Acc. of Scotland.* The bulk are from the *Reports* of the Scottish Typographical Society.

[2] Webb, *Labour in the Longest Reign.*

	1845		1848		1852		1858		1860	
	s.	d.	s.	d.	s.	d.	s.	d.	s.	d.
Glasgow	25	0	25	0	25	0	25	0	25	0
Edinburgh	25	0	25	0	25	0	25	0	25	0
Perth					20	0	20	0	20	0
Montrose.........					20	0	20	0	20	0
Kirkcaldy					20	0	22	0	22	0
Percentage of 1891 wage 79			......		......		79		80	

	1868		1873–4		1875		1877–8		1879–80	
	s.	d.	s.	d.	s.	d.	s.	d.	s.	d.
Glasgow	27	6	30	0	30	0	32	6	32	6
Edinburgh	27	6	30	0	30	0	30	0	30	0
Perth	22	0	23	0	24	0	27	0	27	0
Montrose.........	20	0	22	0	22 0 to 27 0		22	0	——	
Kirkcaldy	22	0	1873, 22	0	1874–5, 23 0		——		25	0
Percentage of 1891 wage 84			90		......		95		95	

	1881–2		1883–90		1891–2		1893		1899[1]	
	s.	d.	s.	d.	s.	d.	s.	d.	s.	d.
Glasgow	32	6	32	6	34	0	34	0	34	0
Edinburgh	30 0 to 32 6		30 0 to 32 6		32 0 to 32 6		32	6	32	6
Perth	27	0	27	0	1891, 27 0 / 1892, 30 0		30	0	30	0
Montrose.........	one member only				25	0	——		——	
Kirkcaldy	25	0	25	0	25	0	25	0	25	0
Percentage of 1891 wage 95			95		100					

The following short table will show the relation of these wages to that of all compositors on the " 'stab."

Weekly Wages in Edinburgh, 1891.　　　Details of Edinburgh rates, 1891.

Books and Weeklies...	32s. to 32s. 6d.,	52½ hours.
Bi-weeklies	32s. 6d.	
Tri-weeklies	35s.	
Morning Papers	40s.,	51 hours.
Evening Papers	35s.,	52½ hours.

It would if space allowed be possible to deal with the provincial towns of England in very much the same way; from 1855 onwards, for instance, following the same plan in the choice of towns, we have　　English rates.

Weekly Time-wages of Compositors.

	1837	1855	1860	1889–92	1893–9[1]
Manchester ...	30s.	30s.	30s.	35s.	35s.
Liverpool ...	30s.	30s.	30s.	34s.	35s. 6d.
Banbury ...		24s.	24s.	26s.	26s.
Darlington ...		21s.	22s.	28s.	28s.

[1] All figures for 1899 and some of those earlier are furnished by Mr G. H. Wood.

A considerable amount of information can be found as to the rate of increase between 1865 and 1885 in the answers to the questions addressed to Trade-Unions in the *Commission on Depression* of 1886 ; and a great deal of miscellaneous information is scattered through the Trade-Unions' reports in the " Webb Collection."

It must be remembered that these wages are those recognised by the Trade-Unions, which have always been particularly strong in the printing trade, and are simply the minimum wages which a member of the Union is allowed to accept, and that in many cases rates considerably higher are paid ; this is the case especially in parliamentary printing during the session.

It will be seen that the wages for printing had risen to a considerable height very early in the century, the rise taking place during the war, when the price of bread was high, but not keeping pace with that price.   At the end of the war the reduction of wages was only partial, and the high wages thus secured have been increased at long and nearly regular intervals—roughly speaking 3s. a week every twenty years.   If the records of wages of all trades were as complete and consistent as these the task of finding an average change of wages throughout the kingdom would be a simple one.

General course.

SECTION XI.

WAGES OF SEAMEN.

THE records of seamen's wages are for the more recent years nearly as complete as those of compositors, thanks to the fact that they have formed the subject of three special returns, (i) *Seamen's Wages* 1867, giving the records for the most important ports and voyages from 1847–66, (ii) *The Supply of British Seamen* 1872, giving similar information from 1847–71; (iii) *Merchant Shipping* 1892, covering the entire period from 1848–91 but not giving all the intermediate years. In the *Returns of Wages from* 1830–86 already often mentioned, extracts from these reports will be found ranging from 1860–86. It is not easy to trace these wages earlier than 1848, in fact the following paragraph contains the only wage statements accessible.

Wages of Seamen.

Data.

In Arthur Young's *Tour in Ireland*[1] wages in Belfast, Waterford, and Cork in 1785 are given as 28s.— 30s. monthly in peace time, and 40s.—60s. in war time, while the average for England is given as 25s. to 30s. in time of peace. From an ordinary observer this statement would be of little value, but Arthur Young's great statistical power and accuracy of observation combined with his experience gathered in all the counties of England in estimating wages and deducing an average from multitudinous observations, make us place more reliance on this apparently casual estimate than at first sight it seems to deserve. Wages for seamen are generally stated as so many shillings per month, and besides

Young, 1785.

---

[1] Hutton's Edition, Vol. II. p. 309.

these wages, board is almost invariably given. This may be taken to be the sort of wage to which Arthur Young refers. We

South Shields, 1817—1833.

next come to a sequence of figures dealing with South Shields[1] from 1817 onwards. Here we find a fairly stationary state of wages in 1817 from 55s. to 60s. per month for distant voyages, a rise to 60s. all round in 1824, a fall of 1s. or 2s. in 1828, and rise to 60s. throughout in 1833, this last statement being confirmed elsewhere[2]. Perhaps we are justified in comparing this with isolated statements by Eden that wages in Sunderland in 1796 were £25 a year, that is 42s. monthly in time of peace, and in time of war from £40 to £100, while in Newcastle sailors received from 6 to 11 guineas in time of war for the month's voyage to and from London. This shows the regular rise during the war found in most trades. Wages at Liverpool were 45s. to 50s. from about 1823 to 1833[1].

Passing now to the general averages found for the period

General, 1848—60.

1848–60 we find them to be 45s. in 1848, 45s. in 1850, 57s. in 1857, 54s. in 1860, and this sequence of figures from 1785 to 1860 shows roughly a rise of 100 per

Value of rations.

cent.; but it must be remembered when dealing with a money wage which is added to board and lodging, that the former may increase at a different rate to the total value of the earnings, and we have no evidence as to the change in value of the rations given to seamen. Since the price of wheat rose in the earliest period we deal with 1785— 1817, we may expect that in this period the value of rations rose as fast as wages; but it is quite possible that since that time the increased quality of the food has not made up for the decrease in its price, in fact from the accounts which are generally given of sailors' food it is hardly possible that they can ever have been worth only half the amount they would have been valued at a few years ago. Since 1860 it perhaps is more reasonable to suppose that the value of the food has kept pace with the less rapid increase of wages, which may be

[1] Committee on *Manufactures, Commerce and Shipping*, 1833.
[2] *Returns of Wages*, Newcastle.

estimated at from 30 to 40 per cent., but information is almost totally lacking on this subject. Where two sets of figures are given, one where food is included, as 70s. a month, and the other a weekly wage where the seamen provide for themselves, the difference since 1860 appears to have been generally reckoned at 10s. a week, and this should be added to their nominal wage when we come to compare their earnings with those members of other industries. An estimate is given on the next page.

The chief difficulty in dealing with these wages however is of quite a different nature. Since 1860 a second set of wages is generally given for sailors employed on steamers, and during this time the number so employed has of course been a constantly increasing percentage of the whole, so that whereas in 1860 only 8 per cent. were on steamships, in 1891 53 per cent. were so employed. Now the wages on steamers have since about 1860 been invariably higher than those paid on sailing vessels on the same voyage, so that we have to make allowance for a constantly increasing number of men paid at the higher rate, in fact to find the average wage at periods since 1860 we must estimate the wage for sailors on sailing ships and sailors on steamships, find the percentage engaged in each, and deduce the average. The figures for the period 1860—1891 appear to be as follows:—

Wages in sailing and steamships.

Average Monthly Wages of Seamen. 1860—1891.

		s.	d.		s.	d.	Weighted Average s.	d.
1860	Sailing ships	54	0	Steamships	64	0	55	0
1870	,,	52	6	,,	65	0	54	6
1875	,,	66	0	,,	74	0	68	0
1880	,,	52	6	,,	65	0	56	0
1886	,,	55	0	,,	68	0	60	0
1891	,,	69	0	,,	86	6	78	0

This shows an increase of 28 per cent. for wages on sailing ships and of 35 per cent. for steamers: but when we come to make allowance for the change in the numbers employed, and for the shifting from the lower to the higher paid section, the total percentage works out as 43. These results are quoted from the paper in the *Statistical Soc. Journal*, 1895, which deals exclusively with wages since 1860. It will be seen then that during the period 1848 to 1891 the wages paid to sailors have increased 50 per cent. in sailing ships alone, or 75 per cent. if we regard sailors in steamships as equally the successors of those engaged in 1848; and if we are justified in accepting Arthur Young's estimate of 27s. 6d. in 1785 it will be found that wages have nearly trebled since then. It must be remembered, however, that these figures refer simply to money wages, and perhaps it is worth while to make an estimate of the difference if we take into account the value of board and lodging. A method very rough, but perhaps not altogether unjustifiable, would be to put this difference as equal to the wages of the agricultural labourer, not that these figures would be exactly the same as the value of a sailor's rations, but that they would increase in nearly the same proportion; we have then the following:—

Rough valuation for food.

Average Monthly Wages of Seamen.

		s.	d.		s.	d.		s.	d.	Percentage
1785	Money wages	27	6	Food	30	0	Total	57	6	44
1850	,,	46	0	,,	40	0	,,	86	0	66
1880	,,	56	0	,,	48	0	,,	104	0	80
1891	,,	78	0	,,	52	0	,,	130	0	100

This correction is of course the roughest of rough approximations, but it shows the sort of alteration we may expect when we make this correction, and in fact wages appear to have about doubled in the century under consideration. Notice however that in comparing the change of wages thus calculated with those in other industries, a special correction would have to be made for the change in the value of money. At first sight it appears that the change in the condition of able-bodied seamen has improved at nearly the same rate as that of agricultural labourers, whose earnings in 1785 were 7s. 6d., in 1891 15s., while the price of a quarter of wheat at the two dates was 43s. and 37s. respectively.

SECTION XII.

SPECIAL STUDY OF WAGES IN THE BUILDING TRADES.

WAGES in the Building Trades form a very useful and interesting study, and accounts of them are very frequent for many districts and periods. To make an investigation extending to the whole country would occupy too much space; attention will therefore be confined to London, Edinburgh and Glasgow. Early records for London are found in an unpublished continuation of Thorold Rogers' *History of Agriculture and Prices in England*[1], where the following statements are found.

Study of Wages in Building Trades. London, Thorold Rogers, 18th century.

Daily Wages at Westminster.

1703–12 Mason, 2s. 6d. Plumber, 3s. 0d. Carpenter, 2s. 6d.
1710–12 Joiner, 2s. 6d.

1703	Bricklayer: 4s.	Man: 2s.		Bricklayer and Man : 6s.	
1704–5	,, 3s.	,, 2s.		,, ,, 5s.	
1706	,, 3s.	,, 1s. 10d.		,, ,, 4s. 10d.	
1707	,, 3s.	,, 2s. or 1s. 10d.		,, 5s. or 4s. 10d.	
1708	,, 2s. 8d.	,, 1s. 10d.		,, ,, 4s. 6d.	
1710	,, 2s. 6d.	,, 2s.		,, ,, 4s. 9d.	
1711	,, 2s. 6d.	,, 1s. 8d.		,, ,, 4s. 2d.	

Meanwhile we find in the Greenwich Records[2] that carpenters, bricklayers, and other artisans were paid 15s. 6d. to 16s. per week from 1710–80. A builder's price book[3], of which the date is probably 1778, gives the following list:

Greenwich Records, 1710–80. Builder's Price Books, 1777.

---

[1] Which Mr A. G. L. Rogers has kindly allowed me to consult.

[2] Macculloch's *Commercial Dictionary*, Art. *Prices*.

[3] Bound between two pamphlets, both dated 1778, in the British Museum, volume 1029. i. 6.

Bricklayer: Lady Day to Lord Mayor's Day, 3s. 6d. per day: labourer, 2s. 2d.
„   Lord Mayor's Day to Lady Day, 3s. 0d.   „   „   2s. 0d.
Carpenter: 3s. 0d. per day, 4d. per hour.
Plasterer: 3s. 0d. per day; labourer, 2s. 0d.; boy, 1s. 4d.
Slater: 3s. 0d.
Paviour: 3s. 0d. or 3s. 4d. per day; labourer, 2s. 0d. or 2s. 2d.

Other Builder's Price Books are extant for many different dates; the object of these publications appears to be to tell a master builder what he may expect to have to pay for labourers and materials for all sorts of work; as we shall see, the wages so found are not always identical with those obtained from other sources.

We obtain the following from Crosby's and Skyring's series of Price Books.

Daily Wages in the London Building Trades, from Price Books.

	Average 1786–1806 Crosby	1806 Crosby	1809 Crosby	1811[1] Skyring	1817 Crosby
	s. d.(d.)[2]	s. d.(d.)	s. d.(d.)	s. d.(d.)	s. d.(d.)
Bricklayer, Lord Mayor's Day to Lady Day	3 9 (5)	5 0 (6)	5 2 (6)	5 6 (7½)	5 0 (7)
Bricklayer's labourer	2 4½ (2½)	3 0 (4)	3 4 (4)	3 6 (5)	3 0 (4½)
Bricklayer, Lady Day to Lord Mayor's Day	3 6 to / 4 3	5 6 to / 6 0	5 6 to / 6 0	6 0	5 6
Bricklayer's labourer	2 9	3 6	3 6	4 0	3 6
Bricklayer, Fire-work	——	——	——	10 0[3]	7s. to 9s.
Carpenter or Joiner, Day	6 9 (5)	5 0 (6)	5 6 (6)	6 0 (7½)	5 6 (7)
Plasterer	3 9	5 6	5 6	——	5 6
Plasterer's labourer	2 4½	3 6	3 6	——	3 6
Plasterer's hawk boy	1 4	2 6	2 0	——	2 0
Paviour	2 2	3 3	5 0	——	5 0
Paviour's labourer	——	——	3 0	——	3 6
Mason	——	——	5 6	——	——
Polisher	——	——	4 0	——	——
Mason's labourer	——	——	3 6	——	——
Plumber	——	——	5 0	——	6 0
Plumber's labourer	——	——	4 0	——	4 0
Slater	——	——	5 6	——	5 6
Slater's labourer	——	——	3 6	——	3 6

[1] Bound up with this at the British Museum (712. h. 6) are piece lists by the Master Carpenters and by the Journeymen, differing a little from each other; Skyring's is intermediate. Of these the *Journeyman's Guide*, which contains piece-rates, estimates average weekly earnings of carpenters at 31s.

[2] Figures in brackets are the hourly rates.

[3] Presumably including a labourer's wage.

	Average 1821 Crosby	1831 Skyring	1848 Skyring	1853 Skyring	1854 Crosby
	s. d.	s. d.	s. d. (d.)	s. d. (d.)	s. d. (d.)
Bricklayer, Lord Mayor's Day to Lady Day.........	5 0	5 0 (d.)	5 3 (7)	5 6 (7)	5 6 (7)
Bricklayer's labourer	3 0	3 6 (4½)	3 6 (5)	3 6 (5)	3 6 (4½)
Bricklayer, Lady Day to Lord Mayor's Day	5 6	5 6	5 9	6 0	5 10
Bricklayer's labourer	3 6	3 9	3 9	3 9	3 9
Bricklayer, Fire-work	6s. to 7s.	7 6	7 0	7 0	6s. to 7s.
Carpenter or Joiner, Day...	6 0	5 8 (7)	5 10 (7)	6 0 (7)	5 10 (7)
Plasterer.....................	6 0	6 0	5 9 (7)	6 0 (7½)	5 8
Plasterer's labourer	3 8	3 8	3 8	3 8	3 8
Plasterer's hawk boy.........	——	——	1 9	1 9	2 0
Paviour	——	——	——	——	5 0
Paviour's labourer...........	——	——	——	——	3 6
Mason......................	6 0	6 0	5 9	6 0	——
Mason's labourer	3 8	3 6	3 6	3 6	——
Plumber	6 0	——	6 0	6 0	6 0
Plumber's labourer	4 0	——	4 0	4 0	4 0
Slater	6 0	——	5 9	6 0	5 10
Slater's labourer.............	3 8	——	3 6	3 9	3 8
Painter	——	——	6 0	6 0	——

In 1874 Simons' *Household Estimator* gives: 1874.

Wages of Bricklayers		
,,	Slaters......	
,,	Masons ...	8½d. an hour.
,,	Plasterers..	
,,	Plumbers ...	9½d. ,,
,,	Painters......	8d. ,,

These wages were a ½d. below the wages just recognised by Trade Unions; whereas in a recent issue of these price books, dated 1893, wages are ½d. an   1893. hour more than those recognised by the Trade Unions for the summer, at which date the wages of most of the artisans given in the above table are 10d. per hour, and their labourers 6d.

Going back to the beginning of the century we find in one of the Place MSS. an interesting account of a dispute between a carpenter journeyman and his master in 1803, respecting an advance in wages, and the award of a Justice of the Peace; an inquiry is made as to the wages that have been paid in recent

Carpenters,
1795—1805.

years in London by various master carpenters and the rapidly advancing price of food is considered; the conclusion is that wages were 18s. in 1795–99, one master stating that five carpenters in his employ were paid 16s., 18s., 19s., 20s. and 21s. respectively at that date; wages rose to 19s. 6d. in 1800, to 21s. or 22s. in 1801, and to 23s. in 1803, in which year the employer had paid six carpenters 20s., 22s., 23s., 24s., 25s., 26s. The Justice held that the plea for an advance had been justified, and awarded a wage of 25s. The Greenwich

1800—1833.

Records give 18s. in 1800, and 30s. in 1810 as the weekly wages of all artisans in the building trades, while in 1820, 1830, and 1840, the wages are stated as 33s.; this statement does not agree with the table already given from the price books, where the wage is up to 36s.; this again is inconsistent with the following information to be found in the evidence of the *Select Committee on Manufactures, Commerce and Shipping* of 1833; there we are told that in London carpenters, joiners, bricklayers, plasterers and painters averaged 28s. from 1817 to 1821, 30s. from 1822 to 1826 (against the 33s. in the Greenwich Records, and 36s. in the Price Lists), and 33s. in the inflation of 1825; this wage was rapidly reduced to 30s. in 1826, and in spite of a strike in that year it remained at 30s. till 1833. The *Report on Artisans and Machinery* (1824) gives similar information as to London carpenters; in 1810 the wage was 26s. to 28s., then a strike raised it to 30s., but it was reduced in 1816 to 28s., and fluctuated between 27s. and 30s. to 1824, when 30s. was the "set" wage. The Report on Trade Unions in the *Social Science Series* (1860) confirms these wages between 1800 and 1818. The *British Almanack and Companion* (1860) gives the following list for London carpenters: 1829, 27s.; 1839, 29s.; 1849, 29s.; 1859, 32s. The *Report on Hand-loom Weavers* in 1838 gives 5s. as the summer daily wage for that year. Comparing these figures it is clear that all

Comparison
of the different
accounts,

except the Greenwich Records and the Price Lists give a uniform series, that shown on the diagram, p. 90; while the Greenwich Records from 1810 onwards and the Price Lists throughout are higher. Now the Greenwich Records are of contract work, and the rates paid to

the masters are naturally higher than those actually received
by the men, while the Price Lists are also of prices charged to
householders by the masters.   The amount of difference between these two rates is illustrated by   and expla-
                                                      nation of their
an account of a dispute between men and masters   divergence.
given in the *Report on Artisans and Machinery*, already
mentioned; it is stated that the men were paid 5s. a day in
1810, but the customers were charged 6s. for their services, and
that in 1816 the rate was reduced to 4s. 8d. for the men, and
5s. 6d. to the customers.   This subtraction of one-sixth part
from the Price Lists harmonizes the figures throughout.

The best evidence we have for the next period is the account
given by Mr Brassey[1] of the great strike in the   Brassey,
Building Trades of 1872, confirmed by the records   1836—1873.
of the Trade Unions.   In 1836 a rise to 30s. took place affecting
first the masons and bricklayers and then the
other artisans.   In the diagram facing p. 90 the   1836.
line showing the course of building artisans' wages indicates the
gradual increase from 1836 to 1847.   The hours at this time
were 60 in the summer and 47 in the winter, the winter hours
being continued for 12 weeks, whereas the former reckoning
from Lord Mayor's Day to Lady Day gave 19 weeks.   In 1847
the hours were reduced to $58\frac{1}{2}$, artisans' wages
remaining at 30s., while labourers received 3s. a   1847.
day.   In 1853 there was a rise of 6d. a day for artisans and 4d.
for labourers; it is not stated whether this was   1853.
accomplished with or without a strike.   In 1859   1859.
one of the great strikes took place, the object being to obtain a
Saturday half-holiday without any reduction in wages and after
the strike the hour system of payment was introduced, the rate
being 7d. an hour, and since two hours were taken off on the
Saturday, $56\frac{1}{2}$ hours were made a week: labourers were paid at
$4\frac{1}{4}d$.   In 1865 wages were raised $\frac{1}{2}d$. an hour for artisans and
$\frac{1}{4}d$. for labourers, and another $\frac{1}{2}d$. was added in 1866, the height
attained being 37s. 9d. per week.   There was a great strike and
lock-out in 1872 with the result that wages were raised to 9d.

---

[1] *Lectures on the Labour Question.*

1873.

in 1873, and hours considerably reduced, namely to 52½ in summer and 48 in winter; the hours in the summer being 9 on Monday, 9½ daily from Tuesday to Friday, 5½ on Saturday. The evidence for the diagrams representing the wages of carpenters or bricklayers is taken from one or other of these sources. In the next few years we are able to follow the carpenters and bricklayers separately. The Operative

Trade Union Returns.

Bricklayers' Society and the Amalgamated Society of Carpenters and Joiners have published complete lists of wages paid in all their branches, since 1867 and 1876 respectively. A general, but rather vague, list is given of wages recognised, in the *Fourth Report on Trade Unions*; here the statement as to weekly wages in 1867, for instance, is " from 37s. 8d. to 18s."; since the maximum rate has always been that in London, we are justified in taking this maximum as being the wage in London. If we were investigating the wages for the trade all over England we should not be justified in assuming that the rate of change had been the same as the change in this maximum, but should have to pay attention to the minimum also, and find some means of connecting the one with the other, but as it is we shall find that this maximum rate tallies with the rates given by other authorities for London. We have then the following list:

1867—1879.   *Bricklayers' Wages in London.*

	Summer		Winter		Rate per hour	Summer hours	Winter hours
	s.	d.	s.	d.	d.		
1867	37	8	34	4	8	56½	51½
1872	39	9	36	0	9	53	48
1876	45	5	39	2	10	54½	47
1879	42	4½	37	10½	9	56½	50½

Of these lines only the first two are given in the table and the method of deducing the others is interesting.

Method of deducing hourly rates and hours of labour.

In the table the hours of labour are given as being, for instance, between 61 and 51: now we cannot of course assume that the maximum number of hours per week was worked in London corresponding to maximum pay, for this is very far from being the case, nor can we be certain that in London the minimum number obtained. Looking back at our other records we find that the hourly rate in 1867 was 8*d*., which by division gives 56¼ in summer and 51½ hours in winter. The hourly rate changed in 1872 from 8*d*. to 9*d*.; it is clear that the figures given refer to the time after the change, for 8*d*. does not divide 39*s*. 9*d*. exactly, whereas 9*d*. does, and gives in fact 53 hours, showing also 48 in the winter. For the rise in 1876 there appears to be no other record than this; it was presumably accomplished by a rise in the hourly rate at the time of the great inflation of trade, but to determine what sum we must consider what number of pence will divide exactly the rate 45*s*. 5*d*.; we thus obtain 10*d*., for 9½*d*. does not divide without remainder, and in every case the figures are given studiously to the exact ½*d*. or ¼*d*. From this we find that the hours were 54½ in summer and diminished to 47 in winter. Applying a similar argument to the wage of 1879 we find that the rate had gone back to 9*d*. (for 10*d*. does not divide 42*s*. 4½*d*. exactly), which gives the hours as 56½ to 50½. There appears to have been no change from this rate between 1879 and 1889, except that there must have been a reduction of hours, for in 1889 we find that hours are reduced back to the level of 1873, while the wage is 9*d*. per hour for 52½ hours in summer and 48 in winter. There was a rise of ½*d*. an hour in 1894 and another ½*d*. in 1895, so that the present wage is 10*d*. an hour; the time of work is 50 hours in the summer, 47 hours for 6 weeks in the autumn, and 44 hours for 6 weeks in the winter; this gives the summer wage as 41*s*. 8*d*. and the average winter wage can be calculated as 37*s*. 11*d*. Similar figures are obtained from 1876 to 1897 for the carpenters, and the result is indicated on the diagram.

1867.

1876-9.

1889.

1895.

Looking back now throughout the century it will be seen that there has been a regular tendency since 1836 towards a progressive increase in wages and a reduction of hours, and that each time the hours have been reduced the hourly rate has been increased to such an extent that there has been no loss in weekly wages. The

Summary for London.

general result appears to be that wages more than doubled
between 1780 and 1897; while since 1830 they have increased
50 per cent., and hours in the same period have fallen 16 per
cent.

A considerable amount of calculation is still necessary to
obtain a complete estimate of the percentage rate
of change in the building trade in London, since
different artisans employed have different rates of
pay, which have not changed at the same dates, and also
work different hours. For instance, in 1876 carpenters worked
52½ hours a week throughout the year at 9*d*., and bricklayers
54½ hours in summer and 47 in winter at 10*d*. In order to
make the calculation complete it would be necessary to know
the proportionate number of these men engaged throughout
London: there appears to be no record of these numbers for
London itself, but there are in many other towns, and a fairly
general idea can be obtained as to the composition of a group
of 100 men, though it varies greatly from place to place. We
also find in many of the records a new class of labourers not
mentioned in the earlier parts of the century who obtain 1*d*. or
½*d*. an hour extra when engaged on scaffolding. We should,
therefore, calculate the wages for 100 men, taking account of
their hourly rate, number of hours worked, number of weeks for
which each number of hours prevailed for each year, and take the
percentage changes; but though this would lead to greater
accuracy it would not make sufficient difference to affect the
general appearance of the diagram on the paper. We will
return to this point after noticing the other towns.

The following table and diagram contain all the available
information as to masons' and carpenters' wages
in Edinburgh and Glasgow: on the whole the
figures form a good continuous record. The chief
gaps are at 1840—1850 for Edinburgh carpenters, where
the absence of records gives no clue to the extent of the rise
which must have synchronized with that of the masons, and
between 1830 and 1850 for Glasgow. Further research may
make it possible to supply these figures.

*The sub-
divisions of
the Building
Trades.*

*Edinburgh
and Glasgow:
masons and
carpenters.*

Summer Weekly Wages of Scotch Building Artisans.

	Edinburgh				Glasgow			
	Mason		Carpenter		Mason		Carpenter	
	Wage	Ref.	Wage	Ref.	Wage	Ref.	Wage	Ref.
	s. d.		s. d.		s. d.		s. d.	
1780–90	——		8 0...... 9		——		——	
1792	12 0......12		9 3...11, 12		——		——	
1794	——				11 0......12		10 0......12	
1800	18 0..... 9		11 6...... 9		——		——	
1804	——		22 0......11		——		——	
1810	17 0...... 8		18 0... 8, 9		22 0...... 1		20 0...... 1	
1811	——		——		17 0...... 2		18 0......1, 2	
1812–16	——		——		18 0..... 2		——	
1812–18	——		——		——		18 0...... 2	
1817	——		——		20 0...... 2		——	
1818	——		——		19 0...... 2		——	
1819	——		——		15 0...... 2		14 0...... 2	
1822	18 0...... 9		——		——		——	
1823	——		24 0..... 9		——		——	
1824	28 0...... 9		24 0..... 9		——		14 0...... 2	
1826	——		14 6...... 9		17 0...... 3		——	
1827	14 0...... 9		14 6...... 9		——		——	
1830	17 0...... 8		——		——		——	
1831	17 0...... 8		——		14 0...... 2		14 0...... 2	
1832	17 0...... 8		——		——		——	
1833	17 0...... 8		——		16 6...... 3		——	
1834	17 0...... 8		——		——		——	
1835	18 0...... 9		——		——		——	
1838	19 0...... 9		20 0..... 8		——		——	
1840	20 0......13		16 0......13		——		——	
1844	20 0...... 7		——		——		——	
1845–7	26 0...... 9		——		——		——	
1848–53	20 0...... 9		——		——		——	
1849	22 0......13		19 0......13		21 0......15		——	
1850	20 0...... 9		——		——		22 0...... 4	
1851	20 0..... 9		——		20 6...5, 15		21 0......15	
1852	20 0...... 9		18 0...... 9		20 6...5, 15		22 0......15	
1853	20 0...... 9		——		25 0...5, 15		23 0......15	
1854	——		——		25 0...5, 15		24 0...4, 15	
1855	24 0......13		20 0......13		25 0...5, 15		24 0......15	
1856	24 0......13		20 0......13		30 0...5, 15		24 0...13, 15	
1857	24 0......13		20 0......13		23 9...5, 13		25 0...4, 15	
1858	24 0......13		20 0......13		25 0...5, 13		25 0...4, 13, 15	
1859	——		——		25 0...5, 13		24 0......13	
1860	24 0......13		20 0......13		25 0...5, 13		24 0...4, 13	
1861	26 0......13		22 0......13		23 9...5, 13		——	
1862	——		22 0......10		23 9...5, 13		24 0......10	

	Edinburgh			Glasgow		
	Mason		Carpenter	Mason		Carpenter
	Wage Ref.		Wage Ref.	Wage Ref.		Wage Ref.
	s. d.		s. d.	s. d.		s. d.
1863	———		22 0......10	23 9...5,13		24 0.....10
1864	———		21 3......10	23 9...5,13		26 0.....10
1865	———		22 4......10	28 6...... 5		26 0.....10
1866	26 3......13		25 6...10,13	27 7...... 5		28 6......10
1867	———		25 6...10,13	28 8...... 5		28 6......10
1868	———		25 6...10,13	28 8...... 5		28 6......10
1869	27 7½......6		26 6......10	27 7½...5,6		28 6......10
1870	———		26 6......10	27 7...... 5		27 7......10
1871	———		26 6......10	27 7...... 5		27 7......10
1872	27 7½......6		27 8......10	29 9... 5,6		29 9......10
1873	———		29 9......10	31 10...... 5		32 0......10
1874	———		31 10......10	34 0...... 5		34 0......10
1875	———		34 0......10	36 1...... 5		36 0......10
1876	38 3...... 6		36 1......10	40 4½...5,6		38 3......10
1877	———		36 1......10	40 4½......5		38 3 10
1878	———		31 10......10	27 7...... 5		34 0......10
1879	———		27 8......10	25 6 . 5,13		27 7......10
1880	25 6...... 6		27 8...10,13	25 6...5,6,13		27 7......10
1881	———		27 8......10	27 7...... 5		29 9......10
1882	———		27 8......10	29 9...... 5		29 9......10
1883	———		27 8...10,13	31 10...5,13		32 0......10
1884	27 7½......6		27 8......10	29 9... 5,6		32 0......10
1885	———		27 8......10	29 9...... 5		32 0......10
1886	29 9......17		27 8...10,17	29 9...5,17		32 0...10,17
1887	———		29 9......10	29 9...... 5		32 0......10
1888	29 9...... 6		29 9......10	29 9... 5,6		32 0......10
1889	———		29 9......10	30 10...... 5		34 0......10
1890	———		31 10......10	31 10...... 5		34 0......10
1891	34 0...6,17		31 11...10,17	32 11¼...5,6		34 0......17
1892	36 1......10		32 11...10,17	35 1.. 5,10		36 1...10,16
1893	35 1......14		32 11......14	36 1...5,14		36 1......16
1894	36 1......16		34 0......16	36 1...... 5		36 1......16
1895	38 3......16		34 0......16	37 2...... 5		36 1......16
1896	38 3......16		36 8 16	38 3...... 5		38 3......16
1897	38 3......16		38 3......16	38 3......16		40 4½ ...16

Authorities:—1. *Weavers' Petition*, 1810. 2. Porter's *Progress of the Nation.* 3. Commission on Manufactures and Shipping, 1833. 4. Nat. Ass. for study of Soc. Sci. *Report on Trade Unions.* 5. Webb's *Industrial Democracy.* 6. Labour Commission, *Final Report*, Part ii. p. 284. 7. Poor Law *Report*, Scotland, 1844. 8. Commission on Hand-Loom Weavers, 1838. 9. *Newspaper Cuttings*, 1853. 10. 2nd, 4th and 6th *Reports on Trade Unions.* 11. *Compositors' Memorial*, 1804. 12. *Statistical Accounts of Scotland*, 1791—4. 13. *Returns of Wages*, 1830—86. 14. *Standard Time Rates*, 1893. 15. *Stat. Soc. Journal*, 1857—8. 16. *Changes in Hours and Wages, annually since* 1893. 17. *Wage Census.*

The Trade Union Reports on the London Building Trades afford material for a specimen calculation of the rate of change of the average wages in a group of occupations from incomplete data. The table facing page 94, which should be compared *seriatim* with the following remarks, gives the rates for five occupations, the weekly and hourly rates having been calculated as already described. The average of summer and winter rates is given where possible, and the average for each year is expressed as a percentage of that for 1897; if we cannot find the winter wage for any dates, it is necessary to calculate a separate percentage line for summer rates, which will be found to have changed at nearly the same rate as the average.

We have then the following figures for certain years :—

London Trade Union Reports since 1859.

Index numbers for each occupation.

Wages expressed as percentages of their height in 1897 for each occupation.

	1859	1867	1872	1876	1879	1890	1897
Bricklayers ...	—	90	94	107	100	94	100
Carpenters ...	—	—	—	94·5	94·5	94·5	100
Painters	87	97	100	100	100	100	100
Plumbers	—	—	—	77	77	91	100
Masons..........	—	91	90	101·5	100	94	100

But since the rates in 1897 were not the same for each occupation, we must before averaging reduce them to a common denominator, thus :—

The same brought into relation with one another.

Wages in each occupation expressed as percentages of bricklayers' wages in 1897.

	1859	1867	1872	1876	1879	1890	1897
Bricklayers ...	—	90·5	94·5	107	101	94	100
Carpenters ...	—	—	—	94·5	94·5	94·5	100
Painters	77	86	89	(100)	(95)	89	89
Plumbers	—	—	—	81	81	95	104
Masons..........	—	90	90	101·5	100	94	100

Here, for example, in 1897 the painter's wage is $\frac{89}{100}$ of the bricklayer's at the same date, and therefore the painter's wage in 1867 is $\frac{89}{100}$ of $\frac{97}{100} = \frac{86}{100}$ of the bricklayer's 1897 wage. For such calculations it is generally useless to calculate beyond the whole number in the percentages; decimal figures should be neglected.

Before combining these figures for a general average it is necessary to form an hypothesis as to the relative numbers employed : for illustration it is here assumed that there are 18 carpenters, 9 bricklayers, 3 masons and 2 painters to each plumber. The wage for 1890 is then compared with that for 1897 as follows:—

"Weighting" the average.

		Wages as percentages of bricklayer's 1897 wage		No. employed				Wages as percentages of bricklayer's 1897 wage		No. employed		
1897	Bricklayer...	100	×	9	=	900	1890	94	×	9	=	846
	Carpenter ...	100	×	18	=	1800		94·5	×	18	=	1701
	Painter	89	×	2	=	178		89	×	2	=	178
	Plumber ...	104	×	1	=	104		95	×	1	=	95
	Mason	100	×	3	=	300		94	×	3	=	282
				33		3282				33		3102

Wage per workman as percentage of bricklayers' 1897 wage

1897.

1890.

$$\text{in } 1897 = \frac{3282}{33} = 99\cdot5\,; \quad \text{in } 1890, \quad \frac{3102}{33} = 94.$$

If there was any change in the relative numbers employed it would be introduced at this stage.

For years between 1872 and 1889 the record for painters' wages is not clear, and it is necessary to interpolate numbers to find the probable rates in 1876 and 1879. Looking at the lists for bricklayers, carpenters, and masons, it is seen that carpenters' wages (as given by the Perseverance Society) show no change between 1876 and 1890, bricklayers' wages rise from 1872 to 1876–7, and return by drops in 1878 and 1889 to the former level, and masons' wages rise less rapidly to 1876, drop in 1880, rise again in 1884, and fall in 1886, but not quite to the level of 1872. The only lists which contain both years agree in a rise between 1872 and 1876; a corresponding rise for painters

Examples of "interpolation."

would bring their figure to 100. Between 1876 and 1879 two lists show stationary rates and two show falls. In order to bring painters' wages to their 1890 level a fall must be supposed, and since this makes the course of their wages agree throughout with that of bricklayers from 1867 to 1890, the best assumption is that the falls between 1876 and 1879 were also in proportion, which indicates 95 as the figure for the latter year. Calculating the average for 1879 as before

$$\frac{101 \times 9 + 94{\cdot}5 \times 18 + 95 \times 2 + 81 \times 1 + 100 \times 3}{33} = 96 :$$

that is, average wages in 1879 were 96 per cent. of bricklayers' in 1897.

No exact law can be laid down for interpolation; all the available evidence must be weighed and regard had to the course of wages in allied occupations. In the table given on p. 91 interpolated figures are placed in brackets. It is because painters have so little weight on the average that the effect of this interpolation is not more marked.

By the same method, the number for 1876 is found to be 98.   *1876.*

Previous to 1876 we have no information to guide us as to the earlier course of wages of carpenters and plumbers. The best method to adopt in such a case is to calculate the change for those occupations for which we have information, and without interpolating any figures, assume that this rate is typical for all. Thus the average of bricklayers' and masons' wages was   **Method when wages are not stated for some of the occupations.**

$$\frac{107 \times 9 + 101{\cdot}5 \times 3}{12} = 106 \text{ in } 1876,$$

and $$\frac{94{\cdot}5 \times 9 + 90 \times 3}{12} = 93 \text{ in } 1872.$$

But the average for all occupations was 98 for 1876. Hence $\frac{93}{106}$ of 98 = 86 is the number to be entered for 1872.   *1872.*

If, however, we had compared 1872 with 1890 instead of with 1876, we should have had

Average wage of bricklayers, painters and plumbers in 1872 : average in 1890

$$:: \frac{94\cdot5 \times 9 + 89 \times 2 + 90 \times 3}{14} : \frac{94 \times 9 + 89 \times 2 + 95 \times 3}{14}$$

:: 93 : 93 ;

from which wages in 1872 and 1890 are found to be equal, and

1872.   94 appears, therefore, to be the average for 1872 since it has been calculated as the average for 1890. It will often be found that by comparison of a particular

Possible
inconsistency
of results.
year with two or three others, that inconsistent results are obtained, owing to the inclusion of different groups of occupations in the different years. In such cases we must either choose the shortest period as least liable to error; or average several periods, or choose that in which most occupations are included. In this case there is much to be said in favour of either method, and

1872.   the general average, 90, has been adopted. It is to be noticed that the closeness of the agreement of the results obtained by the various methods indicates the accuracy which the result may be expected to have.

1867.   By similar methods 87 is found for 1867. For

1859.   1859 our only plan is to take $\frac{77}{86}$ of the average, 87, for 1867, which equals 78; but since painters form only a small and badly paid section of this group of trades, this number must be regarded as doubtful.

We have then the following numbers:

Average Wages of London building artisans, expressed as percentages of bricklayers' wages in 1897.

1859	1867	1872	1876	1879	1890	1897
78	87	90	98	96	94	99·5

These figures are simply proportionate to the average wage,

Reduction to
given base.
which can then be expressed as percentages of that of any year, e.g. 1890, as base; and so we finally obtain:

*Index numbers, showing rate of Change of Wages in the
London Building Trades, labourers excluded, as shown by
the Trade Union reports: the wage in 1890 being taken
as* 100.

1859	1867	1872	1876	1879	1890	1897
83	93	96	104	102	100	106

By methods similar to these the average for any group of
trades can be calculated, great care being necessary
in interpolation, lest a figure resting on doubtful   Generality
evidence should have great effect on the result.   of the method.
Notice that in most estimates of this kind continual attention
should be paid to the estimate year by year of the proportionate
numbers employed, and that when this is done, dying trades
drop out and increasing trades enter automatically.

Such a calculation may appear unnecessarily complex, but
it is the simplest that will automatically introduce all available evidence, and has the crowning advantage of using the
"kinetic" and not the "statical" method, as distinguished
above, and being thus independent of bias in the data employed[1].

[1] For other examples, *vide* the articles by the author, mentioned in the
Bibliography.

SECTION XIII.

COAL MINERS' WAGES.

Complete Sequence of Wages in South Scotland.

THE subject it is now proposed to deal with is one of great
difficulty, and illustrates especially well the
Colliers' wages.
mistakes into which it is easy for anyone, not
thoroughly familiar with an industry, to fall.   There are many
factors to be taken into account before a proper estimate can
be made of a miner's weekly earnings; first the rate per ton
hewn; then the relative value of the rate in a
Difficulties.
particular seam to the general country rate; then
the number of tons hewn in a stint, darg [1], or day's work, or if
the general rate per hour is given, the number of hours'
work at the face; the deductions for weighing and charges
for candles and sharpening picks; the number of days' work
per week, or, as is more generally given, per fortnight; and,
finally, the privileges in the way of cheap coal (often obtained
merely for cost of haulage) and of a free cottage.   All these
are enumerated to show the danger of comparison of two
statements of miners' wages, without a sufficient examination
of the quantities which are included in each case.   A single
omission may easily turn a decrease into an apparent increase.
3s. 6d. and 4s. may be daily rates at successive dates, and are
apparently an increase of 14 per cent., but if the first is earned
for 6 days and the second for 5 days weekly, the weekly rates
are 21s. and 20s., giving a decrease of 5 per cent.

[1] A term which appears to stand for the amount of work which the men
recognize as the normal day's quota.

Before any elaborate investigation into change of wages can be carried out, it is necessary to decide quite definitely as to what course shall be taken in two cases: first, how to deal with a shortening day's work, secondly how to deal with irregularity of work. The coal industry affords the best examples on both questions. There can be no doubt that during the century the normal day's work for the wage-earning classes has diminished very considerably. We have traced this change in the building trades, and the legal reductions in textile factories is a matter of history. In the iron and steel trades reductions have again and again been made, and there is this difference between the course of wages and the change of hours of work, that, whereas in the first case increases and reductions follow one another so that when looking along a line showing the height of wages during the century it is often not clear at first sight whether or no the advance is general, in the case of hours of labour it is very unusual for a reduction once gained to be lost, and the hour-line, if drawn, would be steadily downward. In the building trades, for example, where weekly earnings have increased from 20s. to 40s. in a hundred years, while the rate per hour has increased from 4d. to 10d. i.e. 150 against 100 per cent., is it best to measure the weekly earnings or the hourly rate? It is the first that we should measure for the following reasons: the most definite statement we shall be able to make about an industry is generally, " in one year a workman made 25s. in a normal week; in another 35s." If we have the data we can further say, in the first year he worked, say, 60 hours, in the second 48 for this wage. The value of leisure cannot be measured quantitatively; to some persons it is of negative value, to others the only thing of value. We should only be justified in considering the hourly rate, if each man was at liberty to work as many or few hours as he pleased, and be paid in proportion: but in modern industry each man must generally work till the whole factory stops; though in some engagements a man can take himself away at an hour's notice when he has earned what he wants, yet in a coal mine a man

Methods of treating a decrease of hours, and irregularity of work.

The hour or the week as unit?

must stop at the bottom, whether working or not, till the cage
is ready for him. Even if the circumstances of the work do
not themselves decide how long a man must keep to it, as in
the case of a locomotive engine-driver, yet the opinion of his
co-workers or the pressure of his trade-union may make it
impossible for him to work more than the recognized time:
for if one man works over hours there is great risk that his
time shall become the normal one, without any corresponding
rise of wages. The victories of Trade-Unions have generally
resulted in treaties of this sort; in future the engine shall
run 55 hours a week and that shall be the normal week; the
wages shall be such that the workman can maintain and slightly
improve his former standard of living. The individual has
afterwards no more immediate power to make his week 60
hours at that trade, than to make the solar day more than
24 hours.

Again, if we could be sure that the hours at different dates
represented equal quantities of work, we should be measuring
a fixed quantity (the payment for a fixed output of exertion)
when we are measuring the hourly rate: but as a matter of
fact there is generally no means of comparing the different
exertions required; sometimes the shortening of hours means
a continually greater strain with an output as great in the
shorter as it had been in the longer time; sometimes it corresponds to a change of the nature of the work, as, for instance,
if a needlewoman earned in 8 hours with a sewing machine
more than 10 hours previously with her needle. Even when
payment is definitely for piece work, it is generally impossible
to tell if the work done needs just the same exertion year after
year. At first sight it would appear that the work of hewing
a ton of coal from the face of the rock is just the same now
as 100 years ago, and that we could therefore simply compare
the tonnage rates at any two dates for which they were given;
and indeed the comparison would be in many cases safe, for
the work is still done with the pickaxe; but other circumstances have changed, for as we gradually use our supply of
coal our mines get deeper and deeper; more time is lost going
from the surface (the bank) to the face; while on the other

hand improved machinery may make the journey more rapid, and improved ventilation may affect the fatigue of the work. Apart from this, the tonnage rate is often misleading; for the rate paid varies from mine to mine and seam to seam, depending on the difficulty of getting out particular tons of coal, and this tendency is accentuated in later years.

From these considerations it appears that we should aim at measuring weekly earnings, not the hourly rate. But in applying this rule to collieries we encounter a new difficulty. We cannot speak, in general, of a normal week's work in a colliery. *The normal week in the building, textile and coal industries.* A glance at the "Labour Gazette" will show that the number of days worked weekly varies month by month. *E.g.* the averages given in Feb. 1897, Jan. 1898, and Feb. 1898 are 5·34, 5·06, and 5·24 days per week, a difference of 5 per cent. There is no such thing as a normal week in the coal trade in the sense that there is a 56½ hours week in the textile or a 54 hours week in the engineering trades. The difficulty is slight, but essential. In building, a man gets his full number of hours while on a certain job. If trade is slack the best man will find it difficult, the worst impossible, to get a new job without delay. There will always be a certain number on the unemployed books. In dealing with the building trade, however, we have a definite estimate, the amount of wage of a man in constant employ. We can watch the change through the century of this definite quantity, independently of the regularity of work. This is, in fact, the best quantity to measure,—the change of earnings assuming full work. Regularity and irregularity follow one another in cycles. The problem of time lost can best be studied separately, and it may be found that, whatever may be the appearance in an estimate year by year, the correction for irregularity is frequently not far from nil, when we take decade with decade. In the case of textiles we have still a normal week and its recognized wage: and in making our general estimate for all industries we can enter this wage in its special line, use it as a quantity comparable with an estimate for other trades, and apply if necessary the right correction to the result for the whole sphere of

industry for general want of work; but if we are making an
estimate for textiles alone we must pay attention to the
particular method of dealing with a slack demand: some mills
work half-time, some close, and the supply is gradually diminished till equilibrium is obtained. Now it is the case
with textiles more than with building that the supply of
machinery and hands ready for production tends to outrun
the demand, so that for a few years in succession the full
number of hours is not averaged; and though the difficulty
here does not differ essentially from that in the building trade,
yet in modern times it is less pronounced in the latter. If
we are dealing with a decaying industry the problem is again
different.

To apply the same method to collieries it is necessary either
to compare weekly earnings (including all allowances and subtracting all deductions) year by
year, for which the materials are quite insufficient,
or to compare the day's wage in successive periods, and if
possible decide on the number of days' work in a normal week.
The day's wage is generally the quantity which earlier accounts
give. In each town and district there is a recognised (if not
stated) amount of work that constitutes a day's work. In some
cases it is never exceeded, in others, some men earn more by
more work. It is a sufficiently definite amount for comparative
purposes, bearing year by year much the same relation to the
average of all employed. The question of daily hours is included in it, for at one time the recognised day's work will have
taken say 10 hours, at another, 7, but to this we need not pay
account. The difficulty is the number of days' work put into a
week. One difference between statements of wages apparently
related to the same work is explained in this way, for one
statement may be "the daily wage is on the average 6s."
meaning that one miner with another 6s. is averaged each
working day; another, "the men do not average more than 4s."
meaning that the average for the week, or throughout the year,
is not more than 4s. a day, which would correspond with 6s. for
four days in the week. Supposing then that we understand
the records and that they are correct, how are we to make

The method of estimating colliers' wages.

the comparison? There are two methods open:—one to estimate the number of days' work month by month and year by year, for which material exists in recent years, and say this is the amount which on an average would be earned by men at work all the time the colliery wound coal: this will differ from our method in the building trade, for there we estimated the amount earned on the supposition that full time was worked, letting irregularity of employment have no effect on our result. The other method gives figures more exactly comparable to our general results. Estimate the number of days that are considered at the time and place to constitute full work and assume that a normal week exists however well concealed. Remember that it is only the change in the number of days that would affect our result, i.e. if we *always* assumed an Easter holiday which did not exist, it would not affect our ratio. The change of custom is very slow, one or two good estimates at widely distant periods would be sufficient. Notice any records such as that of the introduction of "Mabon's Day" (a monthly holiday in South Wales[1]): note whether it is customary to work on Saturday and Monday: study the records of normal times, not those of inflation or depression, and there will probably be little doubt left as to whether 8, 10, 11, or 12 days constitutes a fortnight's work. Multiply the daily wage by the number of days' work in a week so determined, and we have the normal week's earnings. Multiply by 52 and estimate the value of a free cottage and coal, and we have annual earnings.

Such an estimate is to be found in J. C. Symons' *Arts and Artisans at Home and Abroad*[2], and is given on the authority of Mr Dixon, a large colliery proprietor in South Scotland.

Colliers' wages in South Scotland.

	Per day		Days per week	Earnings		House		Coal		Net. earnings	
	s.	d.		s.	d.	s.	d.	s.	d.	s.	d.
1811	4	11 ×	4½ =	22	1½	1	2 +	1	5 =	24	8½
1821	3	3	4½	14	7½	1	2	0	9	16	6½
1831	3	11	4½	17	7½	1	2	0	6	19	3½
1838	4	6	4½	20	3	1	2	1	2	22	7

[1] Now abandoned.
[2] And in *Comm. on Hand-Loom Weavers*, XLII. of 1839, p. 530—1.

Here 4½ is probably a rough average of the number of days worked per week.

Wages in South and West Scotland form a very good in-
Wages in South and West Scotland in detail. stance of the method of collating figures, and will well repay detailed study ; the results are shown on the diagram facing p. 106. The earliest figures come from the statistical account of Scotland ; 1791-8. Here, 1792. for 1792, we find such statements as collier's wages in Lanark were 2s. 6d. to 3s. 6d. a day : in Haddington, one collier, with two bearers, in a 3 ft. seam earned 21s. to 25s. a week formerly, and at date of return, with one bearer, in a 2 ft. seam, earns 14s. 2d. In 1794, we find in Haddington £65 annually stated as the earnings of a man with bearers, working 4 or 5 days a week. As we have no later accounts to compare with these of earnings with bearers, the statement that in 1793 in Dunfermline men with no bearers earned 1s. 6d. to 2s. 6d. a day, and men with bearers 2s. 6d. to 3s. 6d., is of great value, showing the worth of the bearers to the man who employed them. We have good grounds for estimating the number of days a week at 4 to 5 from the following list,

Glasgow 2s. 9d. to 3s. per day, £30 annually.

Clackmannan 12s. in 5 days, with wife and daughter.

Haddington with bearers 4 or 5 days a week.

While other statements of earnings are :—Campsie (Glasgow) 1793, 3s. daily; Edinburghshire 18s. to 20s. weekly; Alloa, £25 or £35 annually, and house, garden and an allowance of meal. The value of these allowances can be deduced from the following : Clackmannan 1793, meal at 8½d. instead of 1s. a peck ; house and yard and other bounties to the extent of 30s. annually. From these figures we may estimate the weekly earnings at 3s. a day, 14s. a week, or £30 per annum, for 1791.

The more complete figures from Symons, covering a period of 28 years, are as follows :

Daily wages in South Scotland 1811-39.

1811–12	1813	1814	1815	1816	1817	1818
s. d.	s. d.	s. d.	s. d.	s. d.	s. d.	s. d.
4 11	4 0	4 3	4 6	4 7	4 0	3 8

1819	1820	1821	1822	1823	1824	1825
s. d.	s. d.	s. d.	s. d.	s. d.	s. d.	s. d.
3 11	3 9	3 3	3 6	3 7	4 2	5 3

1826	1827	1828	1829	1830	1831	1832
s. d.	s. d.	s. d.	s. d.	s. d.	s. d.	s. d.
5 0	4 3	4 3	4 3	4 3	3 11	4 1

1833	1834	1835	1836	1837	1838	1839
s. d.	s. d.	s. d.	s. d.	s. d.	s. d.	s. d.
4 0	4 0	4 0	4 9	5 0	4 6	3 6

The Reports on the operation of the Mines Act, 1844 and following years, gives the following estimate for the 'darg':

1825	2 carts at 2s. 6d.
1827	4 carts at 1s. " 5 could have been done."
1837	Strike but no change.
1842	3 carts at 1s.
1844	2 carts at 1s. Young men might take 4s. now.

The question of restricted output has always to be considered in dealing with miners' wages. Colliers have always been ready to limit the output with the idea of keeping up the price, and consequently their earnings per ton. This occurred during the decade 1840–50 and we have the following information:

Lanark: 42 unrestricted earned in a month £189, average 22s. 10d. per week.
48 restricted   ,,   ,,   £175   ,,   18s. 3d.   ,,
Old men, 14s. to 18s.; young men, unrestricted, 18s. to 25s.
,,   restricted, 15s.

In 1843 the wages of certain men were 76s. 4½d., 69s. 7d., 65s., 60s. 6d., 59s. 1½d., 53s. 4d. in one month, giving an average of 15s. 11d. each, per week. In another colliery the average of unrestricted work was 19s. weekly. Other accounts of the 'darg' or day's work are:

Lanark: Sept. 1843—May 1844, 3 carts at 1s. 2½d.=3s. 7½d. per day.
May—Dec. 1844......... 2½ ,,   1s. 5½d.=3s. 8d.   ,,
Aug.—Dec. .... 2 ,,   1s. 6d. =3s. 0d.   ,,

and Lanark: 1844, before April, 8 hutches............ 3s. 0d.   ,,
after ,, 5½ ,, ... 3s. 4d. (6½ hours).

Another account for Ayr in 1845 gives 3s. 6d. daily, with house and coal, equivalent to 19s. 6d. weekly. This seems

comparable with the former series and shows that wages in
1844 and 1839 were equal, while there appears to be no change
in 1843–4.

To carry on the list we have from the Report on Trade
Unions (Association for the Promotion of Social Science):

Scottish miners: 1837   Reduction from 5s. to 4s. a day.

                  1837–42   Reduction to 2s. 6d. and even 1s. 8d.

                  1842–44   Rise of 1s. or 1s. 6d.

                  1844   Fall.

                  1847   Strike: 3s. a day accepted, soon reduced to 2s.

                  1847–50   Remained low, at about 2s.

                  1855   An advance from 4s. to 5s., soon lost after a 16 weeks'
                              strike.

                  1860   4s.

Trade Union Reports[1] give the following series for the
average of the daily wages of all miners in South Scotland:

1851	1854	1858	1859	1860	1861	1862	1863
s. d.	s. d.	s. d.	s. d.	s. d.	s. d.	s. d.	s. d.
2 6	5 0	3 0	3 6	4 0	4 6	5 6	4 9,

less 3d. a day for lights and sharpening picks.

The price per ton being given for one, the Lowthian, colliery
for all years, we should have, if we assumed that a uniform
amount was hewn, the following figures[1]:

1844	1845	1846	1848	1851	1852	1853
s. d.	s. d.	s. d.	s. d.	s. d.	s. d.	s. d.
2 6	3 4	3 6	2 10	2 4	2 6	3 5

1854	1855	1856	1857	1858	1859	1860
s. d.	s. d.	s. d.	s. d.	s. d.	s. d.	s. d.
3 11	4 0	3 7	3 1	3 1	3 3	3 1,

but probably more would be hewn when the price rose.

In 1862 there seems to have been a temporary inflation.

The next series of figures, from Strang in the *Statistical
Journal*, 1858, are confirmatory of these:

1852	1853	1855	1856	1857	1858
s. d.	s. s. d.	s. s. d.	s. s.	s. d.	s. d.	s. d.
2 6	3, 3 6	4, 4 6	5, 4	5 0	5 0	3 0,

while the "Returns of Wages" give 4s. for 1863.

---

[1] Webb's Collection, M.S.S. Miners, I.

Sir Lowthian Bell's account is as follows :—

Daily wages of Scotch Hewers.

1859	1860	1861	1862	1863	1864	1865
s. d.	s. d.	s. d.	s. d.	s. d.	s. d.	s. d.
3 1	3 6	3 2	3 1½	3 7½	4 0	4 1

1866	1867	1868	1869	1870	1871	1872
s. d.	s. d.	s. d.	s. d.	s. d.	s. d.	s. d.
4 6	4 1¼	3 7¼	3 6¾	3 9	4 6	7 0½

1873	1874	1875	1876	1877	1878
s. d.	s. d.	s. d.	s. d.	s. d.	s. d.
9 11	7 2	5 4	4 8	4 1¼	3 2

All these day wages appear to be comparable, Strang agreeing both with Bell and the Trade Union Reports.

The next consecutive list is the account of the sliding scales[1], covering the whole period since 1879; the scale of course gives only the nominal percentage changes, **Sliding Scales.** without the connection with the daily or weekly wage; we must, therefore, find the means of connecting them with the list before 1878. The sliding-scale figures are as follows:

Percentage above (+) or below (−) the Standard fixed at the annexed dates.

1879	Oct.	+18	1887	Mar.	+ 7
	Oct.	+57		July	0
	Nov.	+44	1888	June	− 3
	Nov.	+32		Nov.	0
	Dec.	+20		Nov.	+ 5
1880	Jan.	+32		Dec.	+10
	Jan.	+44	1889	Jan.	+17
	April	+32		April	+12½
	May	+20		June	+16
	June	+ 7		July	+12½
1881	Nov.	+20		Sept.	+25
	Dec.	+ 7		Oct.	+37½
1882	Nov.	+20		Nov.	+50
1883	Nov.	+31	1892	May	+37½
1884	Jan.	+20		Oct.	+25
	Feb.	+ 7	1893	Feb.	+12½
1885	Mar.	− 5		May	0
	Dec.	+ 7		Oct. (or earlier)	+50
1886	Feb.	− 5	1894	June	+25
	June	−16	1895	May	+12½
	Sept.	− 5	1896	March	0

[1] Munro, *Sliding Scales in the Coal Industry*; and Labour Commission, Appendix to *Final Report*.

The estimates of daily and weekly earnings for this period are :

1.   In the comparison of miners' wages, 1871 and 1886, in the *Report* of the Lancashire Mining Federation, the wages for West Scotland are stated to be in 1871, 4s. 6d.; 1886, 4s.

2.   In *Returns of Wages*, 1880.   Hewers 25s. 3d.

3.   In the Fourth *Report* on Trades Unions.   Ayrshire Miners' Union 1887, 3s.; 1888, 3s. 9d.; 1889, 5s. 5d.; it is also stated that the average time worked, when trade was good, was 4½ days per week, 9¼ hours per day.

Trades Union Reports.

4.   In the Wage Census, 1886.   Lanark 17s. 11d. to 27s. 3d., average 22s. 8d.; 48 to 54 hours, bank to bank, 48 hours.

Wage Census.

5.   In the Labour Commission.   Ayr, 1891, 21s. 3d., 45 to 50 hours.   Lanark, 7s. daily; cheap coal and house, 5½ days, 9¼ hours, bank to bank = 38s. 6d.   Ayr, (by Mr Keir Hardie), 4s., 5¼ days, 9¼ hours bank to bank. This is presumably an average allowing for bad trade.

Labour Commission.

The darg is stated to be 5s. 3d. in Ayrshire, 5s. 6d. in Lanark ; while good men earn more.

On the hypothesis that the wage in 1886, which should be 5 per cent. below standard, was 4s. 0d., the standard corresponds to 4s. 2d. a day ; on the hypothesis that the wage in 1890-1, which should be 50 per cent. above standard, was 7s., the standard is 4s. 8d.

Connection of sliding scale with other returns.

The Wage Census average, 22s. 8d. corresponds to 5½ days at 4s. 1½d., making the standard 4s. 3½d.

The Trade Union statements indicate, on the hypothesis that the standard was 4s. 4d., that the differences from the standard were in 1887, −31, in 1888, −14, in 1889, +26 ; but if we assume that the Trade Union rate corresponds to the 'darg' which in 1891 was $\frac{11}{14}$ths of the day rate, these numbers would be

	Day rates	Relation to standard
	s. d.	
1887	3 10	− 12
1888	4 9	+ 10
1889	7 0	+ 62

which are nearer the sliding scales figures.

Lastly, 25s. 3d., the weekly rate in 1880, is, if we reckon 5½ days' work per week, 7 per cent. above standard (which was the case after June), and at 4½ days is 30 per cent. above (which was the case in April). These statements are none of them inconsistent with a standard rate between 4s. 2d. and 4s. 8d., and indicate 4s. 4d. We may therefore carry the list of daily rates by means of the sliding scale year by year on this assumption. The apparent change in the number of days worked needs further investigation.

In using the sliding scale the number of months to which each rate applies must be taken into consideration. Thus in 1881, for 10½ months the rate should be taken as + 7, for 1 month as + 20, and for ½ month as + 9, for a reasonable approximation, and the average for the year as

$$\tfrac{1}{12} \text{ of } (7 \times 10\tfrac{1}{2} + 20 \times 1 + 9 \times \tfrac{1}{2}) = 8\cdot1.$$

As regards individual years we have hardly reached certainty by means of this patchwork; but it will be admitted that by piecing together all this scattered information, we have found figures which may be trusted when averaged over short periods. They are

Daily earnings of a Lanarkshire miner. Result.

1791	1811–20	1821–30	1831–40	1841–50	1851–60
s. d.	s. d.	s. d.	s. d.	s. d.	s. d.
3 0	4 3	4 2	4 0	3 0	3 8

1861–70	1871–75	1876–80	1881–86	1886–90	1891–96
s. d.	s. d.	s. d.	s. d.	s. d.	s. d.
3 9	6 10	4 4	4 6	4 9	5 8

More detailed results are shown in the accompanying diagram.

We have considered the wages of Scotch miners **Other districts.** in detail, because the material exists in greater abundance than for other districts. As the result of a hasty glance at the data for these districts, however, we have the following table, containing part only of the information to hand, which will serve to indicate the course these wages have followed; but these figures have not been examined and compared in detail, and should be used only as a first approximation to the facts.

Colliers' daily wages in various districts.

Northumberland:

1795	1831	1834	1843-6	1849	1861
s. d. s. d.	s. d. s. d.	s. d. s. d.	s. d. s. d.	s. d.	s. d.
2 6—3 0[1]	3 6—4 0[2][3]	15 0—20 0[4] (week)	3 0—4 0[2]	3 6[2]	5 1[4]

1863	1871	1875	1878	1880	1885	1890
s. d.	s. d.	s. d.	s. d.	s. d.	s. d.	s. d.
4 5[5]	5 5[5]	6 5[5]	5 1[5]	5 0[5]	5 5[5]	6 10[5]

Durham:

	1839	1846	1861	1866	1871
	s. d.	s. d.	s. d.	s. d.	s. d.
Daily	3 9[10]	3 9[2]	5 1[4]	5 9[4]	4 10[6]
Sliding scale					82

	1875	1879	1883	1886	1890
		s. d.	s. d.	s. d.	s. d.
Daily		4 2[5]	4 7[4]	4 7[6]	6 0[5]
Sliding scale	104	75	81	77	100

Staffordshire:

1831-40	1844	1847	1848	1849	1860	1871	1886	1891
s. d.	s. d.	s. d.	s. d.	s. d.	s. d.	s. d.	s. d.	s. d.
4 3[4]	3 6[4]	5 0[4]	4 0[4]	3 6[4]	4 0[4]	4 2[6]	3 4[5][6]	6 0[13]

Lancashire:

	1839	1849	1859	1871	1877
	s. d.	s. d.	s. d.	s. d.	s. d.
Weekly	25 0[7]	20 0[7]	25 0[7]		28 7[8]
Daily		4 0[2]		4 6[6]	

	1880	1883	1886	1891
		s. d. s. d.	s. d.	s. d.
Weekly		26 3[8]—27 5[4]		
Daily			4 9[6]	7 0[5]
Sliding scale	100	120	110	150

Yorkshire:

	1844-53	1853	1871	1880	1884	1885	1886	1891
	s. d.	s. d.	s. d.		s. d.		s. d.	s. d.
Daily	3 6[9]	4 0[9]	5 0[6]		4 9[5]		5 2[6]	6 9[13]
Sliding scale				100	107	98	98	138

South Wales:

	1840		1845		1849		1860		1870	
	s.	d.	s. d.	s. d.	s.	d.	s.	d.	s. d.	s. d.
Daily	4	2			3	0[11]	3	0[11]	3 4[11]	—4 11[6]
Weekly	21	0[4]	16 1[4]—19 0[4]		14	3[4]				

	1880	1883	1886		1891	
			s.	d.	s.	d.
Daily			4	7½[6]	6	6[13]
Weekly					39	4[13]
Sliding scale	100	111	104		150	

Weighted ratios, Scotland included[12]:

1840	1850	1860	1866	1870	1877	1880	1883	1886	1891
61	59	68	74	72	75	70	75	71	100

1 Eden.   2 Reports on operation of Mining Acts.   3 Webb Collection.   4 *Returns of Wages*, 1830—86.   5 4th Report on Trade Unions.   6 Pamphlet of the Lancashire Miners' Federation, 1886.   7 Chadwick, *Stat. Journal*, 1860.   8 Levi, *Wages and Earnings*, from Mr Lord's evidence. Comm. on Depression, 1886.   9 Report on Strikes, 1860: Nat. Ass. for Prom. of Soc. Science.   10 *Stat. Journal*, 1889.   11 Dalziel, *Colliers' Strike in South Wales*.   12 *Econ. Journal*, 1898, p. 482.   13 Labour Commission, 1886: 5th Report, Part II., p. 39.

SECTION XIV.

THE TEXTILE INDUSTRIES: HAND-LOOM WEAVERS: WOOL.

IT is necessary to begin the study of wages in textile trades
Earnings of
hand-loom
weavers, 1790
to 1840. with a glance at the Hand-Loom Weavers who
were the most important members of the trade in
the early part of the century. There is no doubt
that the earnings of the hand-loom weavers diminished at an
extraordinarily rapid rate between 1790 and 1840, so that,
whereas at the former date they were a fairly well to do and
contented set of men, at the later date those who remained
were earning a miserable 5s. a week at the expenditure of
14 hours daily work. It is not however easy to determine
exactly the dates and the extent of the fall of their wages,
though it is quite necessary for the purpose in hand. There
are two classes of statements of the earnings of
Relations of
piece-rates to
earnings. these men, one a statement of the piece-rates for
certain lengths of weaving, the other a statement
of their weekly earnings. We must determine whether a
change in piece-rate necessarily meant the same change in
the earnings, before we can use piece-rate changes to represent
changes of earnings. As a general thing it is of course not
the case that piece-rates and earnings change at the same rate,
for a reduction in piece-rates in the era of machinery generally
means an improvement in process of manufacture, and very
frequently that more is earned at the reduced rate than at
the former higher one.

To compare the rates of fall of piece-rates for different goods, take the piece-rates as equal to 100 in the year 1820 and express the rates for the same goods in other years as percentages of the rates in 1820. The date 1820 is simply taken as being one contained in most of the lists given. If a list does not contain this particular year, in order to compare it with the general lists, calculate a base number for some other year, say 1803; thus the lists appear to indicate that the rates in 1803 were 2·6 times those in 1820; we take the number 260 then as the standard for 1803, and express the rates in the lists containing 1803 and not 1820 as fractions of this 260. By this means we can obtain several lists of piece-rates easily comparable one with the other, and so see whether the rate has been the same for all different classes of goods and in different districts or not; we find that the rate of fall has been nearly uniform, varying a little as between England and Scotland. The general result appears to be indicated by the following figures, which do not pretend to exactness:—

1795	1800	1803	1814	1816	1820	1826	1833	1840
400	300	260	220	110	100	50	60	60

Having decided on this list of figures as representing the general rate for piece-rates, next prepare a similar list of figures representing the change in weekly earnings. The best consecutive lists are for Lanark and Glasgow.

Average net weekly earnings of weavers in Lanark[1].

	1795		1800		1805		1807		1810		1813	
	s.	d.	s.	d.	s.	d.	s.	d.	s.	d.	s.	d.
Pullicate ...	21	0	18	6		—		13	6		—		—
Stripe		—		—	21	0	16	0	16	0	11	0

Average net weekly earnings of weavers in Glasgow[1].

	1810–16		1816–20		1826		1832–33		1838	
	s.	d.	s.	d.	s.	d.	s.	d.	s.	d.
Skilled......	20	0	18	0	12	6	10	6	9	6
Inferior ...	10	6	10	3	9	0	7	6	6	0

It will be found that the courses of piece-rates and earnings have not been exactly the same. The reason is generally, not

---

[1] Hand-Loom Weavers, XLII. of 1839, p. 527 seq.

that more was to be earned at the lower prices owing to greater easiness of work, but that the weavers put in longer and longer hours at the same rate of pay, so that their wages fell rather less than the piece-rates, but the difference is not great. The rent of the loom must be deducted to obtain net earnings ; on the whole this rent fell less rapidly than the piece-rates, thus counteracting to some extent the less rapid fall of earnings as compared with piece-rates. Having thus decided that piece-rates correspond fairly closely to the actual fall of earnings, we can estimate these earnings at any dates when we know the

Statements of earnings.

piece-rates that have obtained throughout and the weekly earnings at any one date or for verification two or more dates. For instance we find that at Bolton[1] the earnings were 5s. 6d. gross, 4s. 1½d. net, weekly in 1834, and that the rates then were a quarter of what they had been in 1800 ; from which we conclude that the earnings in 1800 were 22s. gross, 16s. 6d. net ; or, we have the following figures for Glasgow[2]: with the keep of his wife and family a weaver's earnings were respectively 14s. in 1797 and 7s. 6d. in 1834 ; or again, a statement that is perhaps more reliable, that the average in Glasgow[3] in 1812 was for plain goods 12s., and fancy goods 15s. 7d. Combining such statements as these with the lists of piece-rates we shall be able to obtain the actual earnings year by year. The information which it will be necessary to

Authorities.

use in such an estimate is contained in the reports of the *Commission on Hand-loom Weavers* of 1838 to 1840, from which extracts were made in Porter's *Progress of the Nations*, Maxwell's *Manual Labour and Machinery*, Dr Cleland's *Glasgow*, Gaskell's *Artizans and Machinery* and Baines' *Cotton*. A list of the earnings of certain worsted weavers in Yorkshire[4], which though not very representative has every appearance of being genuine, shows that 10s. weekly was made in 1787, that a rapid rise took place to 34s. 6d. in

[1] E. Baines, *History of the Cotton Manufacture.*

[2] Maxwell, *Manual Labour and Machinery.*

[3] Alex. Richmond's evidence to *Select Committee on Artizans and Machinery*, 1824.

[4] Hand-Loom Weavers, XXIII. of 1840, p. 419 seq.

1814, followed by a fall to 12s. 6d. in 1838. On the other hand in Baines's *History of Yorkshire* it is stated that women weavers on power-looms earned 9s. in 1835, increasing to 12s. in 1857, at which date some men on hand-looms were earning 15s[1]. While the hand-loom weavers were decaying all the other branches of the textile trades were increasing rapidly in numbers, and it is doubtful whether with the great dearth of information as to the numbers employed at the various occupations we can so combine the wage statistics as to yield a consecutive account of average wages in textile industries from 1780 to 1830. From the date of the general adoption of the power-loom onwards the problem becomes simpler.

Transition to power-loom weaving.

The best list of wages in the woollen trade is to be found in Baines's *Yorkshire,* but as limits of space prevent the compilation of a complete list of wages in all subdivisions of the work it will be best to look only at spinners' wages. These were high at a very early date, when the spinner was not able to keep pace with the weavers and his services were in great demand. Before the introduction of machinery spinning was of course done by women at their own houses, but as improvements were gradually made the work was taken over by men in the woollen trade, and we find their wages at Leeds to be 16s. 9d. in 1795, 24s. 8d. in 1805, 31s. 8d. in 1815. Soon after this the mule was introduced, the actual difference appearing to be that 'mule' spinners earned 28s. in 1826, while 'jenny' spinners earned only 20s. 4d.; after this wages rose to 25s. in 1835, were 23s. in 1845, and 29s. in 1857. With this we may compare the following from *Returns of Wages*: Leeds mule spinners, 1858, 28s.; 1880 and 1883, 37s. 6d.; and from the Wage Census 31s. 6d. in 1886. It will be seen that the difference in wages between 1805 and the present date is not so great as might have been expected, and even if we look at wages for modern weaving, e.g. 18s. to 24s. at Huddersfield in 1893[2], we find it is not so

Wool. Yorkshire spinners' wages 1795—1893.

---

[1] In 1893 in Huddersfield there were about 55 women to 45 men weavers on power-looms. *Stat. Journal*, 1895, p. 262.

[2] From personal information.

great as the money wage paid at the very beginning of the
century.

Returning for a moment to an earlier date it must be remembered that Yorkshire was not the only, or
perhaps the most important centre of the woollen
trade before the era of machinery, and in fact the *Hand-loom
Weavers' Commission* is occupied with Somerset and Gloucester
almost as much as with Yorkshire. There is a very complete and
reliable table[1] given of wages in all departments in Gloucester-
shire from 1808–38 in factories, and another table[2] shows very
clearly the process of the introduction of machinery. In the first
table we find that master weavers earned 16s. in 1808, falling
to 12s. in 1838 in factories, and 8s. out of doors; while jenny
spinners (women) earned 14s. in 1808, and after the introduction
of mule spinning their wages fell to 12s. before 1828, and to 6s.
in 1838; meanwhile mule spinners (men) earned 25s. from 1819
to 1835 and 22s. in 1836, '7, '8. A very exact table is given of the
classes of labour and amount of wages in spinning: in the period
1781–96 two women were employed at 13s. between them, and
three children at 2s. each; for the same work in 1796—1805 one
woman at 14s. 4½d., one man at 19s. 8½d., and two children at
2s. 6d. each; 1828—38, one man at 15s., and one girl at 3s.
The corresponding changes for weaving at the same dates
were:—master weaver 12s. 3d., with a journeyman at 3s. 6d. and
child at 2s. in the first period; a man at 22s. 6d. and a child at
2s. in the second; a man at 15s. 4½d. and a child at 2s. in the
third.

This slight sketch must suffice here, but material exists for
a complete estimate in Baines's *History of Yorkshire*, and in the
Returns of Wages between 1830 and 1886, which gives wages
in the West Riding from 1855 onwards, while the Wage Census
carries on the information to 1886. In recent times the figures
show a low rate of increase in the woollen as compared with
other trades; thus between 1860 and 1891 the increase appears
to be only 10 per cent.[3].

West of
England.

---

[1] *Parliamentary Papers*, xxiv. of 1840, p. 394.

[2] *Ib.* xxiii. of 1840, pp. 279—281.

[3] *Journal*, Stat. Soc., June, 1895.

SECTION XV.

COTTON.

WAGES in the cotton trade are among the most important and the most difficult to trace: important, both because after those engaged in agriculture and building, cotton operatives form the largest class of wage-earners, and because a majority of these *Peculiarities of the calculation of wages in the cotton industry.* are women, so that here we are able to trace the change in women's wages, which in most other cases is not possible; difficult, because of the continually changing methods of work and payment, the varying nature of the work allotted to each sex, the employment of children under changing legislative restrictions, and the change in nomenclature of the subdivisions of work; difficult and important for the student, because of the mass of apparently inconsistent data existing, the variety of methods applicable to the problem of averaging, and the countless illustrations afforded of the nature of wage statistics. It is not possible in a limited space to do more than state the nature of the problem, and give some illustrations of special difficulties. The chief landmarks in the history of cotton wage-statistics are the general estimate of wages in 1833 to be found in Ure's *Cotton Manufacture,* *Ure, 1833, and the Wage Census, 1886.* which forms the most exhaustive wage investigation of a single industry before recent times, and the Wage Census of 1886. Before 1833 we are dependent on scattered and partial statements in the reports of various commissions; since 1833 we have much valuable information scattered through the Reports of the Factory Inspectors, and general

estimates by Mr Andrew and by Mr Ellison, while Schulze-
Gaevernitz summarizes very ably statistics throughout the
century. For Manchester, in particular, we have very complete
additional information from Lord (*Commission on Depression*),
Chadwick (1839–59), Merttens and Montgomery. The wages
for Manchester are tabulated and summarized at the end of
this section.

Though most of the statements as to cotton wages appear
Complexity   to be reliable in themselves, no greater mistake
of the returns.   could be made than to compare any two wage-
figures without knowing exactly to what district and class of
operatives they refer, and the position they occupy in the main
body of the industry. For wages vary from man to man, mill
to mill, and town and town; from date to date such a denomin-
ation as spinner will include operatives of quite different
character, and at the same date it may mean a spinner of fine,
coarse, or medium yarns, with a difference of 100 per cent. in
wages; this last fact alone accounts for very many apparent
discrepancies. In the case of weavers, the only other class of
workers for which wages are generally given, the difficulty is of
a different nature; the rate earned per loom is easily determin-
able for many dates, but the number of looms worked by each
weaver needs very careful estimation. With regard to workers
in the carding room, who form the third main division of
cotton operatives, the returns are complicated by the varying
number of different processes included in different estimates
under this heading.

In the cotton trade it is necessary to consider all sexes and
Changes of   ages in each estimate, for the work performed by
age and sex.   each is continually changing; children are employed or not as the development of machinery dictates;
women and men often do the same work, or women replace men
as the operations become simplified. For example, the number of
piecers, ' big ' or ' little,' to each spinner, has varied continuously,
and is an important factor in the estimation of average wages.
Besides many minor subdivisions, spinners are now divided into
two main classes, self-acting mule-minders, chiefly men, and
throstle-spinners and ring-spinners, chiefly women; while both

are overlooked by men; any of these may be meant in an average of spinners; in particular, throstle-spinners may be entirely omitted in an average. In the case of weaving the sex difficulty takes a new shape, for both are now employed on nearly identical work, and paid at the same piece-rates, but do not net the same weekly earnings. The gradual change from hand to power weaving, resulting in the main, but with many exceptions, in a complete change of sex, presents yet another series of problems.

It is obvious that a mere statement of the wages of spinners and weavers, male and female, will give a false comparison unless the averages are very carefully weighted. For Manchester we have the following : *Weighting of wage-returns: example.*

	1833 Average wage s. d.	Percentage of total employed in factory	1886 Average wage s. d.	Percentage employed	Per-centage in-crease
Self-acting minders, M.	27 1	15	35 7	5	31
Piecers.............................	5 10	27	12 2	10	10·9
Throstle-spinners	7 7	6	10 5	3	37
Power-loom weavers, M. & F.	10 10	21	13 3	30	22
Average...	12 2		15 2		25

If we applied the 1886 numbers employed to both, the per-centage increase would be 35; the difference is accounted for by the fact that in this table the numbers employed at the higher rates have diminished relatively to the others. The complete result when all employed are taken into account is given below (p. 119). It is to be noticed that neither the wages nor the proportionate numbers employed have followed the same course in other parts of Lancashire, much less in Scotland, where wages are lower and change less rapidly. As far as our purpose is concerned it is fortunate that the cotton industry has never been rapidly and en-tirely revolutionized by the sudden introduction of completely new methods, but that changes have *Description of method of tabulating and averaging.* been introduced gradually, and the alteration in the *personnel* of the workers has proceeded with regularity; this alone makes a system of interpolation possible. The following method appears the only one by which a reliable result can be obtained, while at the same time all available data can be included:—tabulate Ure's estimate and the Wage Census in as nearly as possible the same order; take each little group of subdivisions of work separately, and place in order year by year the data from all sources relating to it, judging from internal evidence exactly to which category (*e.g.* fine, medium, or coarse, spinners) it applies; place all averages given (for all mule-spinners, all spinners, all power-loom weavers, all employed and so on), in their appropriate place, and work out corresponding averages when possible; then by studying the relative numbers employed as stated by Ure and in the Wage Census, strengthened by any intermediate estimates, interpolate numbers for all intervening years, on the assumption that the change has proceeded uniformly; collate all the evidence as to the average number of looms per weaver, and by a similar method of interpolation reduce the statements as to wages per loom to weekly earnings, and calculate general averages; finally, collate the averages for men, women, girls, and lads, wherever given, calculate the same from Ure and the Wage Census; and compare the two series of results obtained. This method is the one adopted in the sequel for Manchester.

The last difficulty which it is necessary to mention is the relation of piece price-lists to earnings. We can-
not simply take the published changes in the price-lists as directly proportional to the changes in earnings, because the rate of earnings changes owing to improving methods, without any alteration in the list; but the price-lists will afford great help in interpolating figures between two good estimates, the dates of sudden change are thus known, and the absence of change will be equally significant.

The use of piece price-lists.

Since the work is chiefly paid at piece-rates, the amount earned in different years is influenced by the operatives' inclinations as well as by the rate of payment; after a period of depression they may exert themselves to make up for lost time; if there is danger of overstocking the market they may relax their efforts. Calculations, therefore, which depend on estimates of piece-rates, and not on contemporary estimates of earnings, may not be reliable as applying to a particular date, but only when averaged to some extent over a normal period.

This consideration applies rather to the question of amount of employment than to rates of wages, and should be treated separately; most piece-work trades present a similar difficulty.

The adjoining table and notes are due to Mr George H. Wood; it must be admitted that the striking consilience of the figures from so many different authorities places their general accuracy beyond dispute. In using the table it should be remembered that Manchester is not a typical centre for weaving, and that the wages are usually for plain weaving, although the class of work done is not always distinguished.

NOTES.

This gives almost every known figure relating to Manchester Cotton Workers. Where so many writers have made estimates it would be expected that a large amount of disagreement would arise, but examination of the figures shows the disagreement to be relatively little. In some cases, Manchester only is quoted, in other cases Manchester and the neighbourhood, the neighbourhood including other places considered in the Wage Census of sufficient importance to have definite tabulations for themselves. Hence in using the figures this qualification must be implied, that they may be applicable to a larger or smaller number of workpeople, according to the area covered by individual investigators in their researches.

The method of arriving at the ratios of advance or decrease as compared with 1833 is explained in the text.

To arrive at the weekly earnings of weavers it was necessary to estimate the average number of looms per weaver, as the rates are given for 2, 3, 4 and 6 looms respectively. The increase in the number of looms per weaver appears to have taken place regularly. The average is not as high in Manchester as in some other cotton centres; Baines in 1833 mentions that most weavers worked 2 looms; in 1886 the average number is only 2½ looms, a preponderance of weavers still working only 2 looms each. There does not seem to have been any sudden change in this respect, and a sliding scale (based on the assumption that the increase has been gradual) has been adopted in obtaining the average wage. This course is justified by the results obtained, as the variations in the resultant average show.

It was more difficult to obtain averages for spinners' wages, but there does not seem to have been any great variation in the proportions spinning coarse, medium, and fine counts respectively, and after successive tabulations of the figures had denoted to which class of spinners the statement referred, the application of weights as shown by the 1886 census gave averages closely agreeing with those arrived at by various writers for the years selected.

SECTION XVI.

THE IRON TRADES.

THE investigation of wages in the Iron trades introduces

The chief divisions of the Iron trades.
several new problems of difficulty, all depending on the rapid evolution and differentiation of these industries, the absence of clear demarcation between the subdivisions, and the hopeless confusion of the returns in the population census. It is not possible here to do more than allude to the main divisions of workers in iron, and deal more particularly with one, viz., mechanical engineering.

Wages at blast furnaces, for puddling, and generally for

Rapid survey of the methods of estimating wages at blast furnaces and rolling mills.
the manufacture of iron and steel, are dominated by the general state of trade, being influenced to a marked extent by commercial depressions and inflations; they are for the most part actually regulated by the market price of iron and steel, and their height from time to time is arranged by a general percentage rise and fall. We must, then, find (i) the percentage changes in the standard rate; (ii) the numerical relation between the standard and the earnings of each class of men (so many shillings wage to each £1 in the selling price per ton); (iii) the proportionate numbers in each class; (iv) the actual distribution of wages at one or, better, two particular dates. Of these, (i) and (ii) may be found in the *Commercial History and Review*, and the *Returns of Wages*; (iii) is often determinate for a single mill, but not for the general industry; (iv) is known only from the Wage Census. The weekly earnings are not, however, directly proportionate to the piece-rates, for in times of inflation a man

earns just what he pleases; in times of depression he can
scarcely make a living; so that the result obtained will only be
correct when averaged over a fairly long period. Lastly, a
number of labourers are employed and paid by workmen, and
their wages do not follow the same course. Similar remarks
apply in the main to rolling mills.

The manufacture of cutlery and tools is a special trade in a
few definite localities; all wages are piece-rates,   Meagreness
of which there are some records, but hardly   of records in
enough to determine weekly earnings, dependent   minor trades.
as they are on the inclinations of the workmen. Similar
remarks apply to nail making and to chain making.

In the latter part of the century iron and steel shipbuilding
becomes of growing importance. A safe and
simple way of treating wages in this industry is   Special
to regard the workers as the successors of ship-   method of
wrights, boat-builders, and perhaps also of rope   treatment of
and sail-makers. The problem is then to be treated in the same shipbuilding wages.
way as the corresponding one relating to seamen in sailing and
steam ships[1]: estimate the wages of each group as accurately
as possible, compute the numbers employed, with the help of the
returns of shipping tonnage built, and combine the results.
Information relating to this industry is to be found in the
*Returns of Wages, Reports of the Depression of Trade Com-
mission*; 4th and 5th *Reports on Trade Unions*; *Wage Census*;
and the volumes in the Webb Collection relating to the Boiler-
makers' Society. The *précis* of Section A, *Labour Commission*,
also, gives useful data for 1891-2.

Workers in iron and steel shipbuilding are very nearly allied
to those in general engineering and fittings shops,   More detail-
the chief differences being in the different relative   ed study of
numbers employed in the various branches, and   general en-
difference in rates of pay for special work. In   Its develop-
general engineering we have our best illustra-   ment and in-
tion of the gradual and increasing specialisation of an industry. creasing sub-division.
The engineer, or millwright, at the beginning of the century
was an all-round man, who often could make the mould, cast

[1] See *supra*, Sec. XI.

the metal, turn, plane, drill and fit, erect the whole machine
or engine and then drive it; his wages were, in 1824, in London
36s. to 42s. a week[1]: while the labourers, the only other large
class of workers, received 18s.; wages in the provinces were of
course lower.   Now the list of occupations is of great and
increasing length, especially in large shops; the Wage Census
gives 53 separate headings for adult labour.   The specialisation
has taken place chiefly since 1840, increasing with the adaptation of machinery to the working up of iron after it leaves the
foundry, the foundry workers being separated from those of the
machine-shop at an earlier date.   In the earlier wage lists a

The evolu-
tion of six
grades of
workers.

single wage-statement might accurately cover the
whole ground, but now several grades of skill have
been developed.   The following figures for Manchester, 1886, are compiled from the Wage Census:—

38s. and upwards:	about 5 per cent:		foremen and a few pattern makers and moulders and smiths.
33s.—38s..........	,, 14	,,	"preference" or highly skilled and specially retained mechanics.
28s.—33s..........	,, 32	,,	ordinary mechanics.
23s.—28s..........	,, 15	,,	machinists, 1st class.
19s.—23s..........	,, 15	,,	machinists and special labourers.
Less than 19s....	,, 20	,,	general labourers.

From this we see that some very skilled workmen are in
receipt of high wages; that mechanics (fitters, turners, erectors,
&c.), who may perhaps be regarded as the successors of the
original 'engineers,' earn the ordinary wages of skilled labour;
and that the application of steam-power to the processes of
milling, planing, slotting, &c., has created a class of machinists,
usually drawn from the ranks of unskilled labour, whose wage
is intermediate between that of general labourers and skilled
tradesmen, and whose work is of corresponding difficulty.   This
grouping seems likely to undergo further developments.

These appear to be the chief points to be borne in mind
when we are compiling engineering wages.   The mistakes to be
avoided are similar to those discussed in the case of cotton.
The problem chiefly depends on tabulation, and of accurate

[1] *Artizans and Machinery*, 1824, 1st *Report*.

weighting by the numbers employed; for the latter material is very deficient, though some figures are to be found in the *Returns of Wages*, and of course the Wage Census gives very complete material for 1886. Good comparative statements are given by Levi, Brassey, Bell, Burnett in the *Claims of Labour*, the *Returns of Wages*, and Lord, in his evidence to the *Commission on Trade Depression*, 1886, and a large amount of useful material is contained in the Trade Union Reports, in the Webb Collection, and in the table giving wages 1862 and 1892 for all branches of the A.S.E., in the 5th *Report on Trade Unions*.

The following table, prepared by Mr George H. Wood, illustrates the use of the material in the case of Manchester :

Tabulation of wages in Manchester.

CONCLUSION.

It now remains to summarize the chief points discussed.

Incomplete-
ness of
material. Our rapid survey is not complete, for many periods of years and many trades are passed by unnoticed. The figures required for our purpose are very plentiful, but are scattered in many books and papers. Many when found are useful, but many more are entirely valueless for the purpose in hand, either because they refer to minor industries for which as a rule consecutive data are wanting, and to write a history of them would be impossible without access to wage books and unpublished records, or because when they refer to larger industries they are couched in too general terms, or are for other reasons not safely comparable Exclusion of
minor indus-
tries, with data collected from other sources. In considering minor industries, however, we may remember that even if we could safely prepare index numbers and its pro-
bably small
effect. for them they could not much affect the average arrived at for such large industries as Cotton, Wool, Iron and Steel, Coal, Agriculture, and Building. It is true that if several of these industries were included it is possible that the result might be altered, because of the large numbers employed in them taken together; but it is improbable that even then the alteration would be great, for the reason that rates of wages in established industries, whether small or large, are governed by the same general causes, and the possibility of gradually shifting from a badly paid trade to a better tends to produce equality in the long run. The complete effect of the changing relative position of industries leads to a problem similar to that of the changing numbers of spinners and weavers; but its satisfactory solution appears almost impossible for want of an industrial census.

The figures discussed here, together with others to which reference has been made, point to the following results, which of course need verification by a much more exhaustive investigation: wages generally increased from 50 to 100 °/₀ between 1780 and the battle of Waterloo, and at one time *General view of the course of wages.* during the war period they reached a very high point indeed. Some trades were able, chiefly through their trade unions, to maintain the pecuniary advantage gained, and in that case their wages are not even now greatly above the rate then prevailing. Retail prices of necessities are however very different, and it is unfortunate that we cannot with safety use index numbers of wholesale prices as a measure of the purchasing power of the workman's wages. A reliable index number of retail prices is urgently needed, and an immense quantity of material for its compilation is procurable from similar sources to those from which wage statistics are obtained.

Further study is needed of wages at 1790 and 1820, *i.e.* before the rise took place and after the period of disturbance had passed. Wages, as is usual in *1795–1820.* periods of inflation, were so variable that no single statement can be relied upon to represent the average for the year. It is the study of normal years that yields the best general result.

Materials are very plentiful for the period 1830–40, chiefly because the prolonged depression of that decade caused so large a number of writers to turn their *1830—1840.* attention to the condition of the wage-earners, and the social questions therewith connected. Indeed material is generally more plentiful for times of depression, or of abnormal inflation (as 1872–4 for instance), than for normal periods.

The study of the period 1830–60 has been much neglected. In it wages in the cotton industry increased about 2*s.* on 10*s.*, although there was a falling *1830—1860.* off until 1845–6. Building trades and town artizans did not improve their earnings by so large a percentage. The wages of seamen increased over 10 per cent. between 1840 and 1860, but the percentage of increase between 1830 and 1840 cannot be accurately measured, except for one port, where they appear to have been stationary. Compositors' wages in small towns increased rapidly but in large towns were stationary, and the average increase was 10 per cent.; those of agricultural labourers increased from 10s. to 11s. 7d., and of miners diminished.

Between 1860 and 1891 increases were very general and averaged about 35 per cent., but the increase was not uniform throughout the period, and the money 1860—1898. wages and real wages took very different courses through the stormy period of the seventies. Between 1891 and 1898 wages on the whole were stationary, except that they have fluctuated in the mining industry, and that in the building trades their rate of increase has come up to the general average. In many cases it is likely that the money wages paid in some year of the inflation of the seventies was greater than any wage since; but owing to the very rapid fluctuation of wages and prices at that time it is not easy to make any useful comparison. It is better to say that money wages in the nineties were 10 per cent. above those of the eighties, and 30 per cent. above those of the sixties. In fact, the following table shows the index-numbers which our work indicates, but which are not yet established :

1780–90	1790–1800	1800–10	1810–20
40	45 to 50	55 to 65	65 to 70
1820–30	1830–40	1840–50	1850–60
65	60	60	65
1860–70	1870–80	1880–90	1890–1899
75	95	90	100

To combine all these various rates ; to allow for the decreasing and increasing importance of various trades; to find changes in the hours of work and constancy of employment ; to estimate the advantage of the increased purchasing power of money ; is a task not beyond the power of statistics, and the material for its accomplishment exists; but at present there is no reliable estimate showing what has been the gain in material comfort in the century of machinery and invention; nor have we more than vague indications of the actual vicissitudes and difficulties of the working classes when the adaptation of old habits to new surroundings was taking place. To bring into true line and position the varying progress and retrogression of the wage earners, and the settlement of the question 'What material progress has been made?' since the time of Eden and Young, the pioneers in such inquiries, is a study of the greatest interest and historical importance, while at the same time it affords a most valuable exercise in statistical method. The object of this book is well fulfilled if it affords any help in such an investigation.

APPENDICES.

APPENDIX I.

TABLE I.

Course of Average Money Wages in selected trades in United Kingdom. Wages in each trade expressed as percentages of their value in 1891. [From the *Economic Journal*, December, 1898.]

Years...	1840	1850	1860	1866	1870	1874	1877	1880	1883	1886	1891
Cotton......................	50	54	64	74	74	90	90	85	90	93	100
Wool	74	79	87	92	97	105	114	110	105	100	100
Building	66	69	78	90	90	98	100	98	98	98	100
Mining	61	59	68	74	72	100	75	70	75	71	100
Iron......................	77	76	80	87	90	103	97	94	100	96	100
Sailors[1]	61	59	70	79	72	90	86	71	82	77	100
Compositors	79	80	83	86	94	95	96	96	97	97	100
Agriculture (England)	75	71	87	90	92	110	112	104	100	94	100

[1] *Vide* p. 80.

COURSE OF NOMINAL WAGES IN UNITED KINGDOM IN SELECTED
TRADES (PERCENTAGE OF VALUES OF EACH IN 1891), FROM
TABLE I.

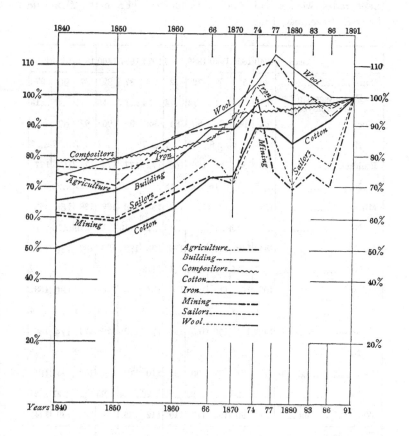

TABLE II.

Comparative Height of Average Money Wages in selected trades in the United Kingdom for various years, the wages of Agricultural Labourers for 1891 being taken as 100, and the relative average wages in other trades and years being estimated by Table I. and the wage census of 1886; and the general weighted average for all these trades (women and children included). [From the *Economic Journal*, December, 1898.]

Years...	1840	1850	1860	1866	1870	1874	1877	1880	1883	1886	1891
Cotton......................	49	52	62	72	72	87	87	82	87	90	97
Percentage No.⎱ of employees⎰	...14	...14	...14	...14	...14	...14	...15	...15	...15	...15	...15
Wool	64	69	76	80	84	92	99	96	92	87	87
No.	... 9	... 9	... 8	... 7	... 7	... 7	...7	... 7	... 7	... 7	... 7
Building	115	122	138	160	160	174	177	173	173	174	177
No.	...15	...15	...15	...17	...18	...19	...20	...21	...21	...22	...22
Mining	111	108	124	136	132	133	138	128	138	130	133
No.	... 9	...10	...13	...14	...15	...15	...16	...16	...16	...16	...16
Iron......................	144	142	150	164	170	193	182	176	187	180	187
No.	...10	...11	...11	...12	...12	...12	...12	...12	...12	...12	...12
Sailors	102	100	119	134	123	151	145	120	139	130	168
No.	... 4	... 4	... 5	... 5	... 5	... 5	... 4	... 4	... 4	... 4	... 4
Compositors	142	144	150	155	169	170	172	172	174	174	180
No.	... 2	... 2	... 2	.. 2	... 2	... 2	... 2	... 2	... 2	... 3	... 3
Agriculture (England)	75	71	87	90	92	110	112	104	100	94	100
No.	...37	...35	...32	...29	...27	...26	...24	...23	...23	...21	...21
Weighted average......	89	90	105	117	119	142	135	129	132	130	144
The same reduced so⎱ that 100 represents⎰ average wage in 1891⎰	61	61	73	81	83	97	94	89	92	90	100
The same when agri-⎱ culture is excluded ⎰	62	64	72	83	83	98	92	88	91	90	100

AVERAGE MONEY WAGES IN THE UNITED KINGDOM (FROM
TABLE II.).

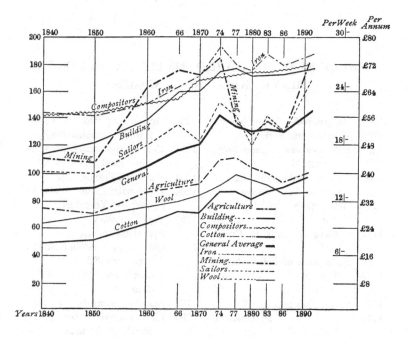

APPENDIX II.

A LIST OF EVENTS WHICH DIRECTLY OR INDIRECTLY HAVE INFLUENCED WAGES.

1764   Hargreaves' spinning-jenny.

1765   Watt's steam-engine.

  ,,   Silk - weavers' procession, Spitalfields.

1767   Tailors' Strike, London; and statute fixing wages.

1768   Arkwright's spinning machine.

1771   Arkwright's mill at Cromford.

  ,,   Federation of Felt-makers.

1773   Silk-weavers' combination, Spitalfields.

1776   Crompton's mule.

1777   Gold beaters' combination, London.

1778   Framework knitters' combination, Nottingham.

1785   Steam-engine in cotton mills.

  ,,   Wool-staplers' new Federal Union formed.

1785 } 1801 }   Cartwright's loom.

1786   London bookbinders strike for shorter hours.

1790   Cartwright's wool-combing machine.

1790   Action against Sheffield Cutlers' combination.

1792   Cotton Spinners' Club, Oldham, established.

1793   War with France.

1794   Combination of Woollenworkers, Yorkshire.

1795   Paper currency.

  ,,   Speenhamland Act.

1796   Cotton Spinners' Club, Stockport, established.

1797   Tailors' conviction, Aberdeen.

1798   Spinning-jenny in use.

1799   Shoe - makers' conviction, North of England.

1800   General Statute against Combinations.

1802   Peace of Amiens.

  ,,   Factory Act, 12 hrs. day in textile industry for parish apprentices.

1804   Edinburgh Compositors' Memorial and fixing of wages.

1806   Berlin Decree.

1807   Orders in Council.

1810   Commercial Crisis.

1810 Commons Committee on London Tailors.

„ Prosecution of London Compositors.

„ North of England Coal Strike.

1811 Luddite riots.

1811–13 Attempts to enforce Apprentice Laws.

1812 Scotch Weavers' Strike.

1812–14 American War.

1813 Statute of Wages repealed.

1814 Statute of Apprentices repealed.

1815 Waterloo.

„ New Corn law.

1816 Demonetisation of silver in England.

„ Stocking Makers' Strike, Leicester.

„ Eastern Counties Bread Riots.

1818–9 Trade depression.

1819 Return to specie payments.

„ Coachmakers' conviction, London.

„ Calico Printers' conviction, Manchester.

„ Ribbon Weavers combine, Coventry.

„ Many prosecutions for combination.

„ Peterloo.

1823 Ropemakers' Strike, Liverpool.

1824–6 Huskisson's fiscal reforms.

1824 Steam-engine makers' Society.

1824–5 Combination law repealed.

„ Seamen's Strike, North of England.

„ Shipwrights' Provident Union, London, established.

„ Organization of Cotton Weavers, Glasgow.

„ Coopers' Strike, London.

1825 First public railway in England.

„ Saturday half-holiday in textiles.

„ Bradford Woolcombers' Strike.

„ Building trade mania.

„ Partial Re-enactment of the Combination Laws.

1825–6 Commercial crises.

1826 Cotton Weavers' outbreak, Lancashire.

1827 General Union of Carpenters.

1828 Carpet Weavers' Strike, Kidderminster.

1829 Manchester Cotton Spinners' Strike.

„ Substitution of hot blast for cold in the iron puddling.

1830 National Association for the Protection of Labour established.

1830 Cotton Spinners' Strike, Ashton.

1830–2 Coal-miners' Strikes, Northumberland and Durham.

1831 Scotch Iron-moulders' Union founded.

1832 Chartism.

„ Reform Bill.

„ Builders' Union established.

1833 Stonemasons' Union.

„ Building Trades' Strike, Liverpool and Manchester.

„ Clothworkers' Lock-out, Leeds.

„ Grand National Consolidated Trades Union established.

1833–4 48 hrs. week for children 9–13; 69 hrs. for young persons 13–18; 10 hrs. day for children in silk mills.

„ Hosiers' Strike, Leicester.

„ Building Trades, Engineers

and Cabinet - makers' Strikes, Glasgow.

1833-4 Cotton Spinners' Strike, Derby.

1834 Factory Inspectors appointed.

" London building trades 10 hrs. day.

" New Poor Law.

" Gasworkers' Strike, London.

" Tailors' Strike, London.

" Case of the Dorchester Labourers.

" Cotton Spinners' riots, Oldham.

1835 Potters' victory, Staffordshire.

1836 Commercial crisis.

" Lancashire Cotton Spinners' Strike (especially Preston).

1836-7 Glasgow Cotton Spinners' Strike.

1836 Engineers' Strike, London; Reduction of hours.

" Ironmoulders' Strike, Glasgow.

1838 People's Charter and Anti-Corn-Law League.

" Select Committee on Trade Unions.

1839 Commercial Crisis.

1840 (circa), power-loom weaving supersedes hand-loom weaving.

1841 Stonemasons' Strike, London.

" Miners' Association of Great Britain and Ireland formed.

1841-2 Depression in textile industries.

1842 Mines Act: prohibits underground work for children.

" Chartist Strikes, Lancashire and Midlands.

1842-5 Peel's fiscal reforms.

1844 Reduction of hours in Engineering Trades, London.

1844 Coalminers' Strike, Northumberland, Durham and Yorkshire.

1844-6 Relay system checked: $6\frac{1}{2}$ hrs. day children, 12 hrs. day women.

1845 Irish potato famine.

" National Association of United Trades established.

1846 Repeal of Corn Laws.

" Railway mania at its height.

1846 London Society of Compositors reorganised.

" Building Trades' Strike, Manchester.

" Coal and iron-miners' Strike, Lancashire.

" Calico Printers' Strike, Crayford.

" Prosecution of Engineers, Lancashire.

1847 Gold discoveries, California.

" $10\frac{1}{2}$ hrs. day in cotton trades.

" Scotch Coal Strike.

" Commercial crisis.

1847-8 Many prosecutions of Trade Unionists.

1848 End of Chartism.

" Railway mania collapse.

1849 Repeal of Navigation Laws.

1850 Tin-plate workers' Strike, Wolverhampton.

1851 Great Exhibition.

" Gold discoveries, Australia.

" Amalg. Society of Engineers established.

1851-2 Amalg. Society of Engineers strike against piecework and overtime.

1853 Preston Cotton Strike: all Lancashire affected.

" Amalgamated Association of Cotton Spinners established.

1853 Carpet Weavers' Strike, Kidderminster.

„ Blackburn Weavers' List.

„ Ironworkers' Strike, Dowlais.

1853–7 Building Trade Strikes, England.

1854–6 Crimean War.

1855 Scotch miners' Strike.

1856 Bessemer steel patent.

1857 Commercial Crisis.

1857–9 Northampton Boot Strike: many strikes throughout the trade.

1858 Yorkshire miners' Strike.

„ N.E. Lancs. Federation of Cotton Spinners established.

„ Flint glass makers' Strikes, Yorkshire.

„ Glasgow Trades' Council established.

1859–60 Building Trades' Strike, London.

„ Chain-makers' Strike.

„ South Yorkshire Coal Strike.

1860 Restriction of male labour under twelve in coal-mines.

„ London Trades Council established.

1861 System of payment by the hour introduced in London building trades.

1861–5 American Civil War and great distress in Lancashire.

1863 Factory Acts extended.

„ National Union of Miners established.

1864 Building Trades' Strike, Midlands.

1865 Puddlers' Strike, Staffordshire.

1865–6 Coalminers' Lock-out, Yorkshire.

1865–6 Shipwrights' Lock-out, Glasgow.

„ Outrages, Sheffield.

1866 Seamen's Strike: inflation of wages.

„ Commercial crisis: failure of Overend, Gurney and Co.

„ United Kingdom Alliance of organized Trades established.

„ Tailors' unions amalgamate.

1867 Regulation of agricultural gangs; minimum age 8.

„ Factory Acts extended.

„ Master and Servant Act.

„ Tailors' Strike, London.

1867–8 Royal Commission on Trade Unions.

1868 First Trade Union Congress.

1869 Amalgamated Association of Miners established.

1870–1 Franco-German War.

1871 Trade Union Act.

„ Criminal Law Amendment Act; repealed in 1875.

„ Engineers' Strike, Newcastle.

1871–4 9 hrs. day widely adopted.

1872–4 Many Trade Unions started.

1872–3 French war indemnity: German sales of silver.

„ Inflation.

1872 (circa), Agricultural labourers' Trade Union—Wages agitation.

„ Gas Stokers' conviction, London.

„ Pattern makers' Association established.

„ Amalgamated Society of Railway Servants established.

1872–6 Women's Unions established.

1873–4 Demonetisation of silver by France and U.S.A.
1873 Regulation of agricultural gangs; minimum age 10.
1874 South Staffordshire and East Worcestershire Coal Strike.
1875 South Wales and Monmouthshire Coal Strike.
„ Conspiracy and Protection of Property Act.
„ Employers and Workmen Act.
1876 Carpenters' Strike, Manchester.
1877 London Building Trades' Strike.
„ Fife and Clackmannan Coal Strike.
1877 Shipwrights' Lock-out, Glasgow.
1878 Failure of the Glasgow Bank and great distress in Scotland.
„ Consolidation of Factory Acts.
„ Lancashire Cotton Spinners' Strike.
„ Bland Act (American Silver).
1879 Lancashire Cotton-weavers' Strike.
„ Trade depression, and want of work.
1879–80 Intense trade depression.
1879–84 Prevalence of Sliding Scales among Coalminers.
1880 Employers' Liability Act.
1882 Ashton Weavers' Strike.

1885–6–7 Depression of trade.
1886 Gold discoveries in Transvaal.
1887 Lancashire Coal Strike.
„ Miners' Federation of Great Britain established.
1888 Matchmakers' Strike, London.
1888–90 Great spread of organization among labourers.
1889 London Dock Strike.
„ Fair Wages clause adopted by the London School Board.
1890 McKinley Tariff.
„ Sherman Act (American Silver).
1891 Amendment of Factory Acts; minimum age 11.
„ Railwaymen's Strike, Scotland.
„ Seamen's Strike, Cardiff.
1892 Shop Hours Act.
1893 Cotton-spinners' Strike, Lancashire.
„ Gold Standard adopted in India.
„ Restriction on dangerous trades.
„ Railway hours regulated.
„ Great Coal Strike.
1893–4 Trade depression.
1894 London Cab-drivers' Strike.
1897 Engineers' Lock-out.
„ Workmen's Compensation Act.
1898 Welsh Coal Strike.
1899 Plasterers' Lock-out.

In the compilation of this table I have been much assisted by Mr Sidney Webb, and have made free use of his History of Trade Unionism; I have also drawn from the tabulation of Factory Legislation in Mr J. A. Hobson's *Evolution of Modern Capitalism*.

APPENDIX III.

BIBLIOGRAPHY.

THE following list contains only the chief sources of Wage Statistics; a more complete one was published in the *Economic Review*, Oct. 1898, where a list, omitted here, of the Trade Union publications, &c. in the Webb Collection at the British Library of Political Science was also given.

The Parliamentary Publications are only distinguished by the Catalogue Volume in the British Museum, which correspond to those in the Library of the Board of Trade. The title is abbreviated by leaving out such words as Commission, Report, &c.; but no difficulty will be found in locating them in the museum, and the title and date are sufficient for finding them in other catalogues. For some recent papers by Command the numbers (e.g. C—6708 of 1892) are given by which they should be ordered from a bookseller.

I. AUTHORS.

ANDREWS, S. Fifty years of Work and Wages in the Cotton Trade. 1887.

BAINES, E. History of the Cotton Manufacture. 1836.

BAXTER, R. DUDLEY. National Income of the United Kingdom. 1868.

BELL, SIR J. LOWTHIAN. The Iron Trade of the United Kingdom. 1886.

BELL, SIR J. LOWTHIAN. Principles of the Manufacture of Iron and Steel. 1884.

BISHCOFF, J.   History of Woollen and Worsted Manufacture. 1842.

BOOTH, C.   Life and Labour of the People.   (In progress.)

BOWLEY, A. L.   Wages between 1860 and 1891.   *Stat. Soc. Journal*, 1895.

     ,,   Agricultural Wages.   *Stat. Soc. Journal*; English, 1898; Scotch, 1899; Irish, 1899; general, 1899.

     ,,   Wages in U. S. A. and Great Britain, 1860—1891. *Economic Journal*, 1895.

     ,,   Wages in France, U. S. A. and Great Britain, 1840—1891.   *Economic Journal*, 1898.

BRASSEY, SIR THOMAS.   Work and Wages.   1872.

   ,,   ,,   Foreign Work and English Wages.   1879.

   ,,   ,,   Lectures on the Labour Question.   1878.

   ,,   ,,   Papers and Addresses.   1894—95.

CAIRD, SIR J.   English Agriculture.   1850—51.

     ,,   Ireland and the Plantation Scheme.   1850.

     ,,   Landed Interest and Food Supply.   1878.

CHADWICK, D.   Wages in Manchester and Salford.   *Stat. Soc. Journal*, 1860.

DALZIEL, A.   Colliers' Strike in South Wales.   1872.

DRUMMOND, SIR HENRY.   Condition of the Agricultural Classes...... from Parliamentary Reports, 1833—40.

EDEN, SIR F. M.   State of the Poor...from the Conquest.   1797.

ELLISON, THOMAS.   Cotton Trade of Great Britain.   1886.

FELKIN, W.   History of Hosiery and Lace.   1877.   (And all other writings.)

GIFFEN, SIR ROBERT.   Progress of the Working Classes.   *Stat. Soc. Journal*, 1883 and 1886.

GIFFEN, SIR ROBERT.   Essays on Finance.   Second Series.

HASBACH, W.   Die Englischen Landarbeiter.   Leipsic, 1894.

HOOKER, R. A.   Wages and Numbers in Coal Mines.   *Stat. Soc. Journal*, 1894.

KEBBEL, T. E.   The Agricultural Labourer.   1893.

Levi, Leone. Wages and Earnings. 1867 and 1885.

McCulloch, J. R. Statistical Account of the British Empire. 1837 and 1854.

Maxwell, John. Manual Labour and Machinery. 1834.

Merttens, F. The Hours and Cost of Labour in the Cotton Industry at Home and Abroad. *Manchester Stat. Soc. Journ.*, 1893—4.

Montgomery, Robert. Manchester in 1834 and 1884. *Manchester Stat. Soc. Journ.*, 1894.

Munro, J. E. C. Sliding Scales in the Iron Industry. *Manchester Stat. Soc. Journ.*, 1885.

Munro, J. E. C. Sliding Scales in the Coal Industry. 1885.

„ „ Coal and Iron. 1890.

„ „ and others. Regulation of Wages in Cotton Industry by Means of Lists. *British Association Report*, 1887.

Porter, G. R. Progress of the Nation. 1851.

Purdy, F. Earnings of Agricultural Labourers. 1861—2. *Stat. Soc. Journ.*, 1861—2.

Schultze-Gaevernitz, G. Von. Social Peace. 1893.

„ „ „ The Cotton Trade. 1895.

Sinclair, Sir J. General Report on Scotland. 1813.

Strang, J. Wages in Glasgow. *Stat. Soc. Journal*, 1857 and 1858.

Symons, Jelinger C. Arts and Artisans at Home and Abroad. 1839.

Tooke, Thomas and Newmarch, W. History of Prices from 1793.

Tuckett, J. D. Past and Present Condition of the Labouring Population. 1846.

Ure, Andrew and Simmonds. Philosophy of Manufacture. Continued by Simmonds. 1861.

Ure, Andrew and Simmonds. Cotton Manufactures of Great Britain. 1861.

Webb, Sidney. History of Trade Unionism. 1896.

„ „ Industrial Democracy. 1897.

„ „ Labour in the Longest Reign. 1897.

„ „ The Condition of the Working Classes of Great Britain. 1842 and 1892. *Cooperative Wholesale Society's Annual*, 1893.

WOOD, GEORGE H. Course of Average Wages, 1790—1860.
Economic Journal, 1899.

YOUNG, ARTHUR. Tour in Ireland. 1776—79.
,, ,,   (Edit.) Annals of Agriculture. 1784—1806.
,, ,,   General View of the County of Herts. 1804.
,, ,,   ,,   ,,   ,,   Norfolk. 1804.
,, ,,   ,,   ,,   ,,   Essex. 1807.
,, ,,   ,,   ,,   ,,   Lincoln. 1808.
,, ,,   ,,   ,,   ,,   Sussex. 1808.
,, ,,   ,,   ,,   ,,   Oxford. 1809.

See also Agricultural Surveys, 1795 to 1815.
Statistical Accounts of Scotland, 1790—1798; 1794—1814;
    1834—1845.
Statistical Account of Irish Counties. 1800—1832.

II. PARLIAMENTARY PAPERS.

Artisans and Machinery ; v. of 1824.
Paying Labourer's Wages out of Poor Rates ; XIX. of 1825.
Silk Trade ; XIX. of 1831—2.
Select Committee on Agriculture ; v. of 1833.
Manufactures, Commerce, and Shipping ; VI. of 1833.
Employment of Children in Factories ; XX. of 1833.
Hand-loom Weavers ; X. of 1834.
Report of Poor Law Commissioners ; XXX. of 1834.
Hand-loom Weavers ; XLIII. of 1839 ; XXIII. and XXIV. of 1840, X.
    of 1841.
Reports on Operation of Mines Act ; XVI. of 1844, XXVII. of 1845,
    XXIV. of 1846, XVI. of 1847, XXVI. of 1847—8, XXIII. of 1850,
    XXIII. of 1851.
Poor Law, Scotland ; XXV. of 1844.
Devon Commission ; XIX. to XXII. of 1845.
Returns of Agricultural Wages ; L. of 1861, LX. of 1862, L. of 1868
    —9, XIV. of 1870, LVI. of 1871, LIII. of 1873.
Women and Children in Agriculture ; XVII. of 1867—8, XIII. of
    1868—9.

Merchant Seamen's Wages; LXIV. of 1867.

Supply of Seamen; LIX. of 1873.

Agricultural Interests (Richmond); XVIII. of 1880; XV., XVI. and XVII. of 1881, XIV. and XV. of 1882.

Depression of Trade; XXI., XXII. and XXIII. of 1886.

Returns of Wages, 1830—86; LXXXIX, of 1887 (C—5172.)

Merchant Shipping Returns; LXVI. of 1890.

Fourth Report on Trade Unions; XCII. of 1890—1 (C—6475.)

Fifth Report on Trade Unions; CII. of 1893—4 (C—6990.)

Sixth Report on Trade Unions; XCIV. of 1894 (C—7436).   1894.

Labour Commission; especially XXXVII. Part II. of 1893 (C—6894, XXIV. and XXV.), XXXVII. part I. of 1893; (C—6894, XVIII. and XXII.), and Appendix to Final Report, XXXV. of 1894. (C—7421, I.).

Factory Inspector's Reports; especially XXII. of 1842, XXII. of 1849, XXIV. of 1866, XIV. of 1868—9, XIV. of 1871, XXVI. of 1888, XVII. of 1893.

Agricultural Statistics, Ireland.   1895 (C—7763) and others.

Wage Census; LXX. of 1889 (C—5807), LXVII. of 1890 (C—6161), LXXVIII. of 1891 (C—6455), LXVIII. of 1892 (C—6715), and the General Report, LXXXIII. part II. of 1893 (C—6889.)

Labour Department.   Changes in the rates of wages and hours of Labour.

Labour Department.   1st Report (1893) C—7567.

"   "   2nd Report (1894) C—8075.

"   "   3rd Report (1895) C—8374.

"   "   4th Report (1896) C—8444.

"   "   5th Report (1897) C—8975.

"   "   Standard Time Rates, C—7567, II.

"   "   Standard Piece Rates, C—7567, I.

III.   MISCELLANEOUS, NEWSPAPERS, &c.

Skyring's Builder's Price Book.   All issues.

London Society of Compositors.   Souvenir, 1897.

The Gorgon, London, 1818—19.

The Beehive.   1869—76.

British Almanack and Companion.   1834 and 1860.

Commercial History and Review.   *Economist.*   Annually Feb. or March since 1862.

Industrial Remuneration Conference.   1885.

Labour Gazette.   Monthly, published by the Labour Department since 1893.

National Association for the Promotion of Social Science.   1858—83.   Especially Report on Trade Societies and Strikes, 1860.

INDEX.

10

146   WAGES IN THE NINETEENTH CENTURY.

Compositors 4, 126, Sec. x. 130—4

Connaught, agriculture 47, 50; building 51

Cooke, Layton 13

Cork, agriculture 47; builders 51; sailors 77

Corn laws 31

Cotton 3, 19, 53, Sec. xv. 130—4

Crosby, building lists 82, 83

Cumberland, agriculture 27, 28, 32, 33, 34

'DARG,' the 96

Darlington, printer 75

Davies, David 25, 43

Derbyshire, agriculture 27, 32, 33

Devonshire, agriculture 26, 33

Dorsetshire, agriculture 32, 33

Druce, S. 28

Drummond, H. 45, 47

Dublin, artisans and labourers 51, 52

Durham, miners 108

EARNINGS and wages 6, 40 to 44, 46, 47
　　,,　　family 7
　　,,　　annual 47

Economist newspaper 13, 120

Eden 13, 25, 37, 61, 64, 78

Edinburgh 14; building 51, 88—90; compositors 71—75; coal 102

Ellison, T. 116

Engineers 52, and *vide sub* Iron

Essex, agriculture 26, 32, 33

FERMANAGH, labourers' diet 47

GAEVERNITZ, Schulze 116

Galton, F. 20, 21, 22

Gaskell, P. 112

Giffen, Sir R. 15, 52, 66

Glamorgan, agriculture, 32

Glasgow 14; building 51, 52, 88—90; coal 102; compositors 71, 74, 75; weaving 111, 112

Gloucester, agriculture 28, 33; wool 114

Gorgon, The 14

HADDINGTON, coal 102

Hasbach, W. 28, 36

Hertfordshire, agriculture 32

Hooker, R. A. 20

Hours of labour 8, 97, 98

Huddersfield weavers, 113

Huntingdon, agriculture 26, 32

INDEX-NUMBERS 91—5

Inglis, H. 14

Interpolation, method of 92, 93

Ireland Sec. vi. 65

Irish Statistical Society 45, 49

Iron Sec. xvi. 130—4

Irregularity of employment 8

JOINERS *vide sub* Building

KEBBEL, T. 28, 39, 43

Kent, 29, 32, 33

Kilkenny, builders 51

Kirkcaldy, printers 75

LABOUR DEPARTMENT, the 16

Labour, fluidity of 19

Labourers' wages 52, 53, 60, 61, 62, 64, 70, 81, 82, 83, 85, 122

Lanark, coal 102—107; weavers 111

Lancashire, agriculture 32, 33; miners 108; textiles 117

Leeds, wool 113

Leicestershire, agriculture 27, 29, 32, 33

Leinster, agriculture 47, 50, 51

Leith 14

Levi, Leone 3, 15, 41, 65—68, 70, 122

Limerick, agriculture 49

Lincoln, agriculture 32, 33

Linen 53

Little, W. 28, 42, 43

Liverpool, printers 75; seamen 78

London, building 81—87, 91—95; labourers and artisans 23, 51, 52, 60, 61; printers 71, 72, 73

Londonderry, building 51, 52

Lord, G. 116, 123

McCULLOCH, J. 14

Printed in the United States
By Bookmasters